PRAISE FOR
THE BEAK IN THE HEART

"Betina Entzminger writes with searing honesty and homegrown lyricism. Line after perfect line, she tells the whole truth about a family of southern women who rebel against patriarchal constraints, hardscrabble women who support each other in order to live with authenticity and misfit integrity. Perhaps the most enthralling story here is the author's own—Entzminger weaves her tale of rambunctious adolescence and experimental parenthood among those of her relatives, both the living and the dead. *The Beak in the Heart* offers inspiration to anyone who ever struggled with family skeletons. In laying out the bones of her kinfolk, Entzminger offers us all a guide as to how we might learn from troubled heritage."

—**George Hovis**, author of *The Skin Artist*

"Weaves vivid portraits of women in her family in a graceful way, dramatic at times, touching, happy and sad. She gives these women distinct voices, and their stories of hardship, injustice, and courage resonate with meaning that links generations from pre-Civil War years to the present. The book is thoughtful, intelligent, and deeply felt—a unique pleasure."

—**Deno Trakas**, author of *Messenger from Mystery* and *Because Memory Isn't Eternal: A Story of Greeks in Upstate South Carolina*

"[Entzminger] discovers several sister dissenters, other women who pushed against the walls of propriety and expectations set up to confine women in the patriarchal South. Telling the stories of the presumed mad women in her family's attics and closets, she shows them sympathy and understanding they did not receive in their lifetimes and gains her reader's (and perhaps her own) sympathy and understanding about her own life choices."

—**Margaret D. Bauer**, author of *A Study of Scarletts: Scarlett O'Hara and Her Literary Daughters*

"I learned not only about the writer's family, but truths about myself and about all women's lives. Wh⸻⸻⸻⸻⸻⸻⸻⸻⸻ed and transformed. Here is the powerfu⸻⸻⸻⸻⸻⸻⸻⸻re is the powerful story of all women."

—**Cherri Randall**, author of *The*

D1490595

the

BEAK

in the

HEART

True Tales of
Misfit Southern Women

BETINA ENTZMINGER

RIVERCLIFF
BOOKS & MEDIA

Rivercliff Books & Media
an imprint of Wetware Media, LLC
RivercliffBooks.com

ISBN: 978-1-954566-07-1

Cover design by Aleksandar Milosavljevic Alek.

Publisher's Cataloging-in-Publication Data

Names: Entzminger, Betina, 1967-, author.
Title: The beak in the heart : true tales of misfit
Southern women / Betina Entzminger, Ph.D.
Description: First trade paperback original edition |
Boulder, CO: Rivercliff Books & Media, 2021.
Identifiers: LCCN: 2021917097 | ISBN: 978-1-954566-
07-1 (paperback) | 978-1-954566-00-2 (epub)
Subjects: LCSH Women--South Carolina--Biography. | South
Carolina--Biography. | BISAC BIOGRAPHY & AUTOBIOGRAPHY
/ Personal Memoirs | BIOGRAPHY & AUTOBIOGRAPHY
/ Women | HISTORY / United States / State & Local / South
(AL, AR, FL, GA, KY, LA, MS, NC, SC, TN, VA, WV)
Classification: LCC CT3262.S65 E58 2021 | DDC 975.7/043/082--dc23

To my parents, with love and with thanks for all the stories.

And to my children.

Contents

"Take thy beak from out my heart,
and take thy form from off my door!"
Quoth the Raven "Nevermore."

—Edgar Allen Poe, *The Raven*

Prologue

With each keystroke, I hear my father's admonitions repeating in my head: "What will people think? Don't tell everything you know. Be careful what you put in writing."

Secrets are secret for a reason. They are often shameful, and they have the potential to hurt others. But buried truths can fester. Once I was in a car accident, breaking the passenger side window with my head. At the emergency room, I asked the doctor if he couldn't just leave those slivers of glass in my scalp. They weren't really hurting much, and I thought they'd just heal over. He laughed and told me they were sure to get infected and then I'd just have more problems later on.

Like those embedded slivers, buried secrets can produce their own toxins that damage not just our bodies, but also our minds, spirits, and relationships.

When I was a child of six, my older sister, about twelve then, resentfully asked our father why she was not allowed to do something our thirteen-year-old brother could do. I don't remember what she wanted to do, and that isn't the important part of this memory. The important part is the reason she couldn't: my father impatiently replied, "Because you're a girl and he's a boy! There are some things that boys can do and girls can't! That's just the way it is, and you might as well get used to it!"

What truly implanted those words in my long-term memory was hearing my mother, later that day, replay the scene as an amusing anecdote to a neighbor lady, saying "And he was right. It's good to learn that now!"

My thought at the time was an unarticulated mixture of: "Why? That's not fair!" And, toward my mother, "You're a girl, too! Why are you laughing?" Today, I would frame my response using terms like "double standard" and "injustice."

That same sense of injustice that frustrated me at age six also inspires my fascination with the women who occupy the following stories. They were my near and distant, maternal and paternal relatives living in Columbia and Blythewood, South Carolina, between the 1850s and 2018. Mostly poor, uneducated, disempowered, these women were either voiceless in their time or their voices were not long heeded. These are not the Southern ladies who were hoisted, willingly or not, onto pedestals by Southern gentlemen. These were the women who grew and cooked those ladies' food, cleaned their clothes, and milled the cloth for their dresses; or they did this work for their own families while their husbands labored at low-paying jobs.

They are all misfits for their time and place. And these women are me. That same sense of injustice leads me to tell their secrets, and some of my own.

I am grateful for the privileges that make my life different: higher education, higher income, relative power and the ability to share my voice. As a senior in high school, I received a full scholarship to the University of South Carolina, and eventually I earned a Ph.D. in English from the University of North Carolina at Chapel Hill. Today, I am an English Professor at Bloomsburg University, a public liberal arts college in Pennsylvania. Yet I am aware that my privileges were made possible in part by my female relatives' rebellious assault against their society.

My ancestresses' lives reveal sadness and suffering, but also strength and endurance. Even in their voicelessness, misery, and lack, dignity remains. Restoring their voices is my attempt to pay homage to them, acknowledge my spiritual kinship to them, and draw from their stubborn strength.

But I have more selfish motives as well. By examining these women, I hope to better understand myself. It's less painful to poke at others' wounds than one's own, and I hope their stories will help me understand why I have always failed to fit comfortably in my Southern home, a place I love and hate with passion, why I have held such conflicted feelings toward male authority figures, starting with my father, and why I have married and divorced four times.

I've changed the names to protect the privacy of my relatives. I tell you their stories, sticking to the facts that are available, but filling in the details that silence and time require from imagination, so you can see them, too.

In some cases, you will clearly know when I speculate, but in other cases, you'll wonder. Where fact and fiction collide, I hope to inspire the imagination and create tension, to encourage you to ponder the biases of the historical record and the possibilities of shifting realities that depend on one's perspective. I am an unreliable narrator in part because memory itself is unreliable, and in the Southern vernacular, telling stories is the same as lying.

— 1 —

Victoria's Mark

...And so maybe if you could go to someone, the stranger the better, and give them something—a scrap of paper—something, anything, at least it would be something just because it would have happened, be remembered even if only from passing from one hand to another, one mind to another, and it would be at least a scratch, something, something that might make a mark on something...

—William Faulkner, *Absalom, Absalom!*

From about 9:30 in the morning until almost noon of that warm August day, I sat in the tidy, air-conditioned living room of the family genealogist; I'll call her Rosa. In the center of one wall, a picture window dressed in white sheers and a heavy floral valance admitted filtered sunlight and a partial view of the park across the street. The other walls bore enlarged black-and-white photographs of Rosa's parents and grandparents from the first half of the twentieth century. An oil portrait of a nineteenth-century ancestress, with lovely brunette hair and a vibrant teal dress, sat in a gold-colored frame on a side table. Rosa told me she had had this portrait made from a photograph of the original painting, which had been slashed by Sherman's troops during the Civil War. A partial wall of open display shelves, featuring ceramic birds, dogs, and ball-gowned ladies, formed the border between the living room and dining room, and two cabinets in the dining room held delicate china and pink Depression glass, the inherited treasures of several households. The house was quiet save our voices, but the faint smell of a litter box revealed the presence of a silent, unseen cat.

I sat on a comfortable sofa; Rosa sat on a straight-backed chair pulled over from the dining table, and a low, oval coffee table stood by our knees. On the table rested a large, embossed, bone-colored Holy Bible and a copy of the maroon, hardback genealogy book that had been Rosa's life's work. I had asked for this meeting with Rosa in Columbia, South Carolina, in order to research the writing project I would pursue during my sabbatical from Bloomsburg University in Pennsylvania, where I taught English.

Particularly, I wanted to talk about Thomas W. Whitman (1815 -1891), a planter and slave owner reputed to have had a long-term relationship with one of his slaves, Victoria, a liaison which produced one or more children. I first learned of this ancestor and his family while reading Rosa's genealogy. When I had spoken to Rosa on the phone, she seemed enthusiastic about the visit, suggesting I find a particular court case about our distant relative in the South Carolina Archives and mentioning a note someone had given her long ago.

"I'll show it to you if I can lay my hands on it ahead of time," she said in a honeyed Southern accent.

By the time of our meeting, however, something had changed.

"What is it you want to know?" she asked.

I wanted to know more about Thomas and Victoria's relationship, about the children they shared, about how each of them felt about their union, and about Thomas's wife. As I explained my interests again, I sensed her defensiveness.

"There's simply no documentation to prove it. I think you've jumped to a wrong conclusion." Rosa impatiently pushed back the short iron-gray hair that curled around her pale face.

"You don't think that Victoria and Thomas had a relationship?"

"Who knows? Besides, it's no one's business."

My cell phone buzzed with an unexpected call. As I reached to silence it, Rosa suspiciously asked, "Are you taping this?"

"No," I said.

Rosa explained that Thomas's papers had all been destroyed during the "Confederate War." Oral history of African-American Whitman descendants links Thomas to Victoria, but there's no real documentation. Emancipated slaves often took their owners' names, Rosa elaborated, so a shared surname doesn't always indicate shared DNA.

"The gold standard for research is three separate sources, such as wills, census reports, or other written records. We don't have anything like that."

She complained of someone sharing *her* research online and sharing her email address. The genealogy book she'd self-published a few years ago had begun four decades earlier as a high school project, so she was understandably possessive of its contents. After it came out, she'd gotten emails from Victoria's descendants asking her for more information about their ancestors.

"There's just no proof," she said.

Here are the gold-standard, documented facts about Thomas W. Whitman. Born in 1815 in Blythewood, South Carolina, he grew up in his uncle Peter Whitman's house, but it is not clear which of Peter's brothers or sisters was his parent. Probably he was the illegitimate son of an unmarried sibling. Upon his death in 1855, Peter left his nephew his entire estate, "consisting of Lands, negroes, [and] Stock of Every description." But Thomas was already a property owner before his uncle's death. The 1850 census lists the value of Thomas's property as nearly twice that of the landowners living near him. He also owned eighteen slaves, thirteen men and five women ranging in age from five to forty. By 1860, he had two fewer slaves, possibly due to a typhoid epidemic that had swept his property in 1856 or '57 and made Thomas sick as well. No names are associated with these enslaved people, only tick marks next to their age and gender, so it's impossible to know if these same sixteen had also lived on Thomas's land ten years earlier.

Was Victoria one of the slaves indicated by tick marks on the 1850 and 1860 census records? Was Thomas's first child one of these marks as well? There were two slaves in 1860 who could have been the right ages to have been both Thomas's relatives and his property: a twenty-year-old woman and a three-year-old male child. The three-year-old must have been a child of one of the slaves; someone so young would not have been purchased on his own. But what was his name, and who was his father?

We continued to talk, and Rosa gradually became more comfortable as we looked over her book together and pulled up census records on her laptop. She enjoyed the pursuit of facts and the opportunity to instruct, and she examined the figurative puzzle pieces I set before her, pointing out those that fit and those that did not. Although she was only about fifteen years my senior, she punctuated her comments to me with "baby," or "honey," or "child." But as I packed up my notes and prepared to leave, she issued a frosty warning. I was not to use her name in print or quote her.

"If you do," she said archly, "I will haunt you to your dying day."

My parents' house is only a block and a half from Rosa's, and I walked back down the street feeling sticky from the humidity. My mother and father have lived in the same house for more than sixty years. It's a brick ranch, originally with two small bedrooms and one bathroom, which they added on to the year I, the third of their four children, was born. When I was a child, a wisteria vine grew in the corner of their yard, and I loved its perfumed purple flowers. The vine is long dead, and my father has created a makeshift parking space for visitors in the corner of the yard where it used to stand. I walked through the pine needles and dried magnolia leaves that paved this spot to where my mother and father sat on the front porch.

I grew up in a quietly racist household. The N-word was not used in our home. No ancestor or currently living relative that I'm aware of belonged to the Klan or participated in racially motivated violence. Yet I learned that black and white people should lead separate lives. *Gone with the Wind* was aired on television yearly, and watching it together was a special event. My family's church and my neighborhood kindergarten were completely white, except for the custodians. I never interacted with black children until I went to first grade. I remember returning from my first day and reporting with pleasant surprise that a slightly older black girl had helped me reach the monkey bars during recess.

"She was nice to me," I told my parents.

"Don't have too much to do with them," my father said.

Gradually, I learned that interracial romantic liaisons were shamefully taboo. As a teenager and young adult who loved to push boundaries, that was one I didn't cross. My father sometimes suspiciously inquired about the racial identities of boys I asked permission to go out with, but they were always white. Once I teasingly asked my mother what she would do if I wanted to date a black boy. "I'd have your head examined," she replied.

As times have changed, my parents have had to adjust their views to accommodate a biracial great-grandchild (my great-niece), whom they love; but I, at fifty-two, am still afraid to tell them about my middle-aged, biracial boyfriend in Pennsylvania.

As we went inside to lunch, I told my mother and father about my visit with Rosa and my research in the archives from the day before.

"Rosa just wants to keep family matters private, especially if they aren't complimentary," my father suggested.

Unlike Rosa, they didn't seem to mind that I was asking these questions of the distant past, yet, like Rosa, they didn't have the answers that I wanted most. Was Victoria's relationship with Thomas consensual? How long did it last, and how many children did they have? Did it continue throughout Thomas's two-year marriage during the Civil War? Did his wife know, and how did she feel?

"He probably slept with a lot of them," my father offered. "Who knows how many mixed children he had?" He was implying that all white men of Thomas's stature did this.

As I searched for satisfying answers, I encountered a frustrating, concrete blankness of which I had long been aware in the abstract: most of history is the story of white men.

✦ ✦ ✦

"Maybe she caught his eye during the typhoid epidemic. She would have been about seventeen then—an attentive nurse, strong and vital amidst the sickness and death?"

"Maybe," I said.

I was back in Pennsylvania, talking to Jerry about my trip and my research. We had been dating for over a year by then, and as I sat on his sofa puzzling over Victoria's story, my pale fingers intertwined with his dark ones. A few years older than me, Jerry is a fellow professor, poet, Navy veteran, and father to two grown children. He was born in Pennsylvania to a white mother and a black father. My parents knew nothing about him because all of his wonderful qualities would not compensate in their eyes for the fact of his racial heritage.

"I wish I could find some treasure trove of plantation records," I lamented, "or the diary of somebody who knew her. But it doesn't exist."

We commune with some of our dead through documents, photographs, and stories, but some stay buried in silence forever.

Although Victoria left no written records, I believe I sometimes hear her voice. She has at times inhabited my dreams like a Fury, the mythical Greek creature of guilt and vengeance. In these visitations, I become aware of a shadowy female figure standing just behind me, outside of my line of sight. I sense that she may be terrible to look at, like Medusa, so I dare not turn to face her. She is angry and, although I can't discern a word she speaks, I have a sense of being hectored by her. "Find out!" I believe she wants to say. "Tell!"

Yet telling has its own anxieties. Another recent dream involves visiting my parents' house, entering the formal living room that they use only for company. Proudly, my mother shows me that they have redecorated, and in my dream I somehow know that they've done this work in preparation for handing the house down to me. But I am aghast at the new décor. I see the ancient, brown, nubby-upholstered couch from my earliest childhood that in reality had been retired long ago. This and other threadbare, scuffed, and frayed furniture sits on a dirty, snagged gold carpet that extends up the side of each wall by three or four inches, the way some cheaper hotel-room carpets do.

Furious, I shout at my mother and gesture emphatically with my hands. "Why on earth would you do this!? Didn't you think I'd want to decorate it myself? Didn't you know I like the hardwood underneath?" Somehow I know the wood floor has been ruined by the hideous carpet glued on top of it.

Angrily venting my dream rage at my eighty-four-year-old, white-haired mother, I am horrified to see her frail chin drop, her mouth cringe open, and her eyes squeeze shut as she begins to sob.

"We just wanted it to be nice for you!" she wails. I am seized by guilt for my ingratitude and meanness, but the dream ends before I can utter another word.

The dream stems from my conflicted feelings of loyalty and indignation, with the house representing my family and its past, and the carpet representing the "official" versions of history and the careless forgetting that obscure the lives of some family members. I'm offended at this obfuscation of truth by time, yet I know that it was often done in a misguided attempt to make things "nice" or simple by people who lived before my parents' time. Also, I acknowledge that by exposing some secrets, I may betray those who covered them over in the first place.

But why does Victoria occupy so much psychic space for me? Recently, I purchased and completed a commercial DNA test that informed me that, somewhere far down the line, I have an African ancestor (research for another time and another story), but I am not a direct descendant of Victoria and Thomas. He was my first cousin, four times removed, a contemporary of my great-great-grandfather. If their society had recognized their relationship, Victoria would have been my distant cousin-in-law.

Part of my interest stems from the way my parents talked about interracial relationships when I was growing up. My adult resentment of those sentiments urges me to shed light on the hypocrisy buried in family history. More than that, though, I believe that an injustice has been done. By refusing to publicly acknowledge his and Victoria's offspring, Thomas and his white relatives denied these children and their descendants their birthright, humble though it turned out to be. What Thomas did is only a microcosm of what the South did as a whole to African Americans in the nineteenth and early twentieth centuries. I don't believe that Thomas was a horrible man; he was an average man for his place and time, but that does not excuse the wrongs he committed. Finally, as a feminist, I strive to create gender balance by exposing those imbalances in the past, by providing a voice to those whom history denied their gold-standard, documented existence.

✦ ✦ ✦

Victoria is not the only woman in Thomas's life whose story has been lost to time. In 1862, when he was forty-seven years old, he married a local girl, Elizabeth, age twenty-four, the stepdaughter of a Confederate general. But this war bride was not long for the world. She died childless in 1864 of unknown causes. If family legend is true, however, Thomas did manage to produce a child, if not a legal heir, while married.

Census evidence and oral history confirm that Victoria had three, possibly four, children: William (born about 1858), Susan (born about 1861), Adeline (born about 1863), and Henry (born sometime between 1865 and 1872). But about the children's father, the historical record is murky. Rosa threatened to haunt me to my dying day, but I wish that Victoria's ghost would come to tell me the secrets that history has omitted from its pages.

Like much of the South, Thomas Whitman suffered financially as a result of the Civil War. By 1888, three years before his death, he was involved in a court case over the rightful ownership of his land due to his excessive debt. I read the transcript of this case in the state archives. In the testimony, one claimant to his property, Dr. Samuel Bookhardt, discussed Thomas's "way of living" as an indication that he had been a poor manager of his property. He accused Thomas of "squandering the property on those Negroes," and of having a long-term affair with a black woman: "They have a grown child. They must have been living in adultery many years."

When we spoke in her living room, Rosa pointed out to me that the man who accused Thomas of this conduct was trying to discredit him. Others had testified to his managerial skill without mentioning such a liaison. Perhaps this testimony is not reliable. In fact, Thomas remarks at another point in the testimony that he has no children of his own.

But the day before my meeting with Rosa, at the South Carolina Department of History and Archives, I had talked with one of the archivists, also a distant relative. Seeing what I was interested in, he brought me a folder of material he had collected over the years. He especially pointed out a handwritten note on a torn piece of notebook paper.

"Rosa gave me that," he said.

The note, signed by one of Thomas and Victoria's recent descendants, said that Thomas W. Whitman had a long-term relationship with his house slave, Victoria, and that they had a child together, named Henry. This must have been the note that Rosa mentioned on the phone, but when I went to her house, she didn't bring it up. I don't believe she forgot about it; I think she decided not to share it. Sensing her defensiveness, I had made a conscious decision not to ask.

Similar information was available on a popular genealogy website, and I had even come across a document that I don't believe Rosa possessed. Online I found a Social Security application made in the name of Henry Whitman, a black man born in 1872, listing Thomas Whitman and Victoria as his parents. Wasn't this proof?

✦ ✦ ✦

Rosa isn't the only family member to have written a genealogy. A descendant of Thomas and Victoria, Thomas A. Whitman, Jr. published a genealogy of African American families in New York in 2002. In it, he lists two children, William and Susan, from the union of Thomas W. Whitman and Victoria in South Carolina. In 2018, this descendant of Thomas and Victoria's collaborated with other Whitman descendants to revise another genealogical publication. They added Adeline, the child born during Thomas's marriage to Elizabeth, as the offspring of his relationship with Victoria. Strangely, these books don't mention Henry, the only descendant about whom I've found a historical record that identifies Thomas and Victoria as parents.

Some facts seem certain: The 1870 census lists Victoria living next to Thomas W. Whitman, with William (eleven), Susan (eight), Adeline (seven), Henry (five), and two younger children (Alex and Eddie) in her household. By 1880, William was living nearby with his wife, and they had named their first-born son Thomas, perhaps after William's father.

So who was Henry? Was he another man's child, even though his is the only birth linked to Thomas Whitman by historical document? When was he born? The 1870 census indicates he was born in 1865, the 1880 census indicates 1867, but the social security application that links him to Thomas and Victoria lists his birth in 1872. Could these be three separate Henry Whitmans, all living in the same neighborhood, and all with or near Victoria?

Through a genealogy website, I've made contact with three of Thomas and Victoria's descendants, two of whom are descended from William, one descended from Adeline. With one of these descendants—I'll call her Mrs. McCannon—I've corresponded several times, trying to solve the mystery of Henry.

"I've never heard of Henry, but the other siblings were mentioned all the time when I was growing up," she said. "Maybe she was caring for a neighbor's or relative's children when the census takers came by."

Quite possible. The 1870 census does not list the relationships of the various household members, only their names and ages, but this theory still leaves the annoying remainder of the Social Security application. Of course, people lie on records all the time, due to mistrust of the government or in order to join the military or receive Social Security benefits early. And former slaves, especially the many like Victoria who couldn't read or write, may not have been certain of their ages. Before the era of computers or even effective records—death certificates weren't kept in the US until 1915, and birth certificates weren't ubiquitous until after World War II—verifying these facts wasn't easy.

Assuming some inaccuracies in dates, I can account for Victoria until her death in 1917, and for Henry until 1940, when he disappears. In 1900, for example, Henry Whitman lived with his wife and children, next door to Victoria, in the Blythewood area, so I am convinced that she was his mother.

Family legend among African American Whitmans has it that Victoria moved to Virginia for a time and came back. Mrs. McCannon also told me that Victoria eventually married a Black man named Andrew Salley, and with this information, I was able to track down records of her later life. The 1900 census lists Victoria Salley, age fifty-five, living alone next door to Henry Whitman and his wife and children in Blythewood, South Carolina. The 1910 census lists Victoria (age sixty-seven) and Andrew Salley living together in a house in that same area. I chalk up the mathematical inconsistencies to Victoria's uncertainty of her own age or to inaccurate guesses on the part of the census takers. `

In 1917, Victoria Salley, age eighty according to the birth year on her stone, died in the same neighborhood in which she had been enslaved. I do believe, though, that Henry finally got away. According to a 1920 census, Henry Whitman learned to read and write, and by 1924, he and his wife had moved to Baltimore, Maryland.

+ + +

On my visit to Columbia, after I'd met with Rosa and had lunch with my parents, I drove my mother and father to visit family graves in Blythewood. My father especially likes to see these markers of his ancestors' existences, but he doesn't drive much anymore. Our first stop was Sandy Level Baptist Church, where the graves of near and distant relatives dating back to the early nineteenth century surround the white church building. As we strolled the graveyard, I paused in front of my parents' granite gravestone, which they bought and had erected several years ago to save their children the trouble. Already engraved on it are their names and birth dates. A blank space awaits their dates of death.

From there, my father directed me about a mile down the highway to a small Whitman family graveyard, located in the edge of the woods on what was once the corner of Thomas Whitman's land. I couldn't have found this place on my own.

We parked in the grass on the road's edge and walked a short distance through the trees, my parents using canes to traverse the rough and unfamiliar terrain. I held my mother's arm as we crossed fallen limbs and ducked under hanging vines, looking for the gravestones. After a short search, we found the worn, lichen-covered monument for Thomas's Uncle Peter, erected shortly after his death in 1855, and next to it, a newer one for Thomas, erected within the last ten years by the South Carolina Department of History and Archives. No one knows for sure that his body actually rests beneath this stone, but there is evidence of several graves in the area, marked by sagging earth and cantaloupe-sized rocks placed where the head and feet might lie. Who else lies beneath the ground here? Thomas's mother? Lizzie? Victoria's relatives? I can only imagine. As we strolled around in the leaf litter swatting gnats, I tried to count the dead.

"This is probably the last time I'll ever make it out here," my father said somewhat mournfully, looking frail in the dappled sunlight among the trees and stones.

Our last stop was a place my parents had never been before. Just down the highway from the Whitman family graveyard, in a plot of land originally deeded to former slaves by Thomas Whitman, lies Little Zion Baptist Church. My mother and father chose to wait in the car while I surveyed the churchyard. They both had trouble with their legs, and walking had already tired them out, but they also feared they wouldn't be welcomed by the several black church members gathered at the front of the building.

I parked the car in the lot behind the church and walked around to the front of the building. A small group of men and women were cleaning up after what appeared to have been a bake sale or church picnic. The smell of barbecued meat lingered in the air. I approached the man who seemed to be in charge, and, after coming to a pause in his conversation, he looked over at me.

"Would it be alright if I looked through the cemetery?" I asked.

"Go on," he said, waving his hand toward the graveyard beside the church and quickly returning to his chat.

A few paces inside the brick and iron fencing, facing the highway, a large granite stone bears the name of Victoria Sally on the right, and of her daughter Susan on the left. Just behind it stands a much older stone for Victoria's daughter Adeline. Like Thomas's, Victoria's stone was erected, without the "e" in Salley," long after her death, by Susan's daughter, Delia. The actual location of her final resting place is uncertain.

The inscription Delia chose for her mother and grandmother's marker suggests a hope for the righting of earthly wrongs in the afterlife, from the biblical book of Thomas: "In my father's house are many mansions." I hope Victoria resides in one of them.

But gravestones, like all writing, address the living. They etch names in history, impeding the corrosive forces of selective memory and time.

And, so, I add these scratches on paper to Victoria's mark.

— 2 —

Correspondence

Is that what writing amounts to?
The voice your ghost would have, if it had a voice?

—Margaret Atwood, *MaddAddam*

Several years ago, when I was visiting my childhood home for the holidays, my father gave me a box of treasure. We walked down to the basement where, in a makeshift office, he kept two file cabinets filled with papers. The room smelled of mildew, and a fine layer of dust coated the furniture. The purplish indoor-outdoor carpet that had been there at least forty years, soaked by flooding during many heavy rains and left to "air dry," clashed with the yellow-painted cinder block walls. Dad's National Guard group picture, circa 1955, hung on the wall, and he asked if I could tell which of the young men was him. I had seen this black-and-white photo many times before, and I remembered his position on the risers: top row, last on the right. But that twenty-something-year-old man still looked like my father, or at least the father I remembered from childhood. Standing trim at six feet and with baby-blue eyes, he was a handsome man despite the small, pitted acne scars on his cheeks. He wore his thin, dark hair short, parted on the side, and slicked down with water.

On this day in December 2012, he had invited me down to the basement to show me the file drawers where he kept his financial documents so I could one day assist my older brother in settling his estate. Every bank statement for the last fifty years lay neatly bundled by year with rubber bands that had lost their snap. But the bottom drawer of one cabinet held genealogy research and a small wooden crate, labeled "Roast Beef, Product of Argentina," which contained old letters and other keepsakes my father had inherited when his father died about forty years earlier. Among them were a small pocketknife, broken metal-framed eyeglasses, and a set of dentures that had belonged to my great-great-grandfather, Jeremiah Winfield Whitman. Most of the letters had been written to my great grandfather, William Warren Whitman (1875 -1949), and to his second wife Kitty (1875 -1944). To me, they seemed like unearthed booty.

"Are you sure you don't want them anymore?" I asked.

"Yeah," he said, sitting on a stool. Eighty years old, he sometimes lost the feeling in his legs if he stood too long. "I'm not going to do anything with them. I always meant to, but now I'm out of time." His voice cracked at these last words, and he teared up. Embarrassed, he covered his eyes with his hand and sat silently until he regained composure. My father saw death standing patient but near; my throat tightened with fearful awe, and my eyes stung with unshed tears at the enormity of this recognition. But we are not a family of huggers. Instead, I touched his shoulder awkwardly and said, "It's okay," or something equally meaningless.

I believe that was the first time I'd seen him cry. I've seen it once or twice since then, and I believe this new emotionality is a by-product of encroaching dementia. I had always thought of my father as a hard person, both difficult and insensitive; whenever I wanted to fight or cry, he always told me to control my emotions.

I think he liked to be thought of as hard. In fact, shortly after this vulnerable display, when I was back home in Pennsylvania, he called me on the phone to reassert his tough, crusty identity. I'd sent Mom a Macy's gift card for her birthday in January, and Dad complained.

"Don't send us gift cards anymore. It's not convenient. They get your money and then we *have* to go to their store. I thought I'd told you that before."

"You did tell me before," I replied. "But I didn't send it to you. Mom likes to shop."

"Well, don't do that anymore, you understand me? We don't want to drive across town. Send money if you want to."

I spoke only to my father that day; Mom remained silent on the subject. She had learned to hold her tongue in their sixty years of marriage. Angry, I called him a bully. He habitually browbeat Mom, who wouldn't stand up to him, and he tried to intimidate his children, even long after they'd become adults. With this call, we reestablished our normal, tense relationship.

But I am grateful to him for trusting me with these old letters from his basement file. They speak to me; I will keep them and try to groom one of my children to accept them someday. I am surprised that they have been preserved this long, handed down over three generations.

My great-grandfather, William Warren Whitman, was a South Carolina corn and cotton farmer of modest means, who sold patent medicine for the National Remedy Company on the side—not the type whose papers are usually thought to have historical value. He married his first wife, Lula May, in 1900, and together they had five children. I have a picture of the pair together, attractive, young, dressed in formal clothes with high collars, seated for the portrait. Both have dark hair; Lula May wears hers piled in a loose bun on top of her head, and William sports a large mustache. In a later photo of William alone, he stands facing the camera with two prized possessions: a revolver in his right hand, over his heart, and a silver pocket watch, suspended from a vest button by a strap.

From what I can glean from the handful of letters to and about William, he too was a hard man. I imagine he thought of emotions as a luxury or a weakness, and, though he felt them deeply, anger was the only one he openly indulged. For example, he scrawled one note, the only note written by him in my collection, on the inside of a 1911 F. S. Royster Guano Company calendar. The paper bears dark spots from ink or age around the faded cursive. The note reads:

De the 20, 1911

Mother died and said to her boys to be good to each other and Be good to Albert. She died at 4:15.

This note is a study in contradictions. On the one hand, William logged the exact time of his mother's death and her dying words. She wished her adult sons to treat each other well. To have recorded these details suggests a touching sentimentality. On the other hand, he wrote this expression of love on a used fertilizer calendar, albeit one that he saved and passed on to his son, who passed it on to his son, who passed it on to me. Here was a sign of devotion, thrift, and practicality: a free promotional calendar turned tribute, bat shit in memoriam.

Apparently, he did not write a similar expression about his wife Lula May's death in 1917. Instead, he saved a typed letter from the local farming supply merchants, offering their sympathy for the family's loss: "Of course it is hard to understand things of this kind, but no doubt there is always a reason and let's remember he who reigns above never makes a mistake."

According to her official death certificate, "he who reigns above" had caused Lula May to, in the coroner's words, "just drop dead" at the age of thirty-five, seemingly from "heart failure," leaving her husband to tend the farm and five children, age sixteen, twelve, ten, eight, and one.

For the next several years, William Warren had trouble paying his debts. He saved several bills from the owner of the general mercantile with increasingly insistent requests for payment. In 1921 and 1922, this sum was $14.60, but in 1923 it jumped to $214, which would be close to $3,000 today. Finally, the owner took him to court to collect payment.

William's insolvency was at least partly beyond his control. The twenties didn't roar for South Carolina due to the post-war changes in the market, a boll weevil epidemic, and poor farming methods that exhausted the land. And William's family never recovered their financial stability. Throughout the years, he took out loans against tracts of land and, during the Great Depression, received food distributions from the Department of Public Welfare.

But I believe he was more than just a victim of agricultural disaster; I believe he was lonely, too. Around 1924, he married for the second time. Kitty, a widow with three grown children of her own, became his wife and the stepmother of his children, the youngest of whom was about seven. Bride and groom were both almost fifty.

The majority of the letters my father gave me are between Kitty and her oldest child, Lizzie, who lived in Charlotte, North Carolina. Their comments about William suggest a marriage that sometimes strained like pine trees against the wind. William was a controlling man, but the fact that he kept these letters suggests that he loved his second wife deeply, even if he didn't know how to show it. On the other hand, Lizzie, whose father had died about two years before her mother remarried, missed Kitty and disapproved of her new relationship. I see a subtle battle for possession between William and Lizzie, written with invisible ink between the lines.

Among the collection of letters was one written to Lizzie by her sister-in-law, Clara:

Correspondence

Dear Sister,

Your letter read and very glad to hear from you but very sorry indeed to hear of your mother getting married. What on earth does she mean? But I guess she knows best. I thought she would marry him. I told Walter she was going to marry and it made him so mad. That was before we left Columbia. What do you think about it? I guess you do get lonesome there by yourself.

I have me a cute bathing suit, shoes, and cap. I am going to the beach this afternoon. It's just like July down here. We stay in the water half the time. I have gained 4 lbs.

I don't have any idea when we will ever come back there. I don't want to for that is such a awful place. Walter said to tell your mother to please send $215.00 as he didn't have any money to pay his board with and said as soon as he went to work he would send it back. Well, as I don't know anything to write I will close.

Clara and Walter

How did this letter, written to Lizzie (who lived in Charlotte) by Clara (who lived in Miami), come to be among those passed down by my great-grandfather (who lived in Blythewood, South Carolina)? When did he read it, and what did it make him feel?

My father once said to my brother, "Be careful what you put in writing. You never know who might read it." He issued this warning after my brother, about age fifteen, found a cassette tape hidden away in a basement lock-box. He managed to open the box and play the tape while my father was at work, and then he played it a second time for me. At this age, my younger brother, having grown larger and more practical than me, and having inherited a masculine need to protect, often treated me as if I were the younger one. In this household from which our two older siblings had fled, we were allies.

On the tape, we heard a recorded phone conversation between my father and the secretary in his office at Southern Bell Telephone Company. Recording the call would have been relatively simple with a cassette player and an accessory that attached to the phone receiver like a suction cup, sold at Radio Shack for such purposes. My father's tape-recorded voice was too breathy, obviously nervous, as he wished her a happy birthday.

"Oh, Frank," she said, sounding like a Betty Boop cartoon, "you're getting me all hot and bothered. I'm going to have to take a cold shower."

We didn't know why he recorded the conversation: as a memento? Because he thought he might one day need or want to prove to others that some liaison had occurred between them? But strangely, at that time, we didn't really wonder why. We were surprised about the tape's contents, but the fact that he had recorded a compromising phone conversation and preserved the evidence did not seem odd to us at all.

I didn't read the note my brother left on the kitchen island for my father that night, but I know it expressed his anger at my father's documented indiscretion and his tight-fisted control over his teenage children, which seemed hypocritical in light of this tape. The note was an adolescent captive's reckless, self-righteous attempt at blackmail.

"Be careful what you put in writing," my father said, calling his bluff. "You never know who might read it." What he meant, without having to say it out loud, was, "You wouldn't want to hurt your mother, would you? How would you feel if she read this?" To my knowledge, the cassette was never mentioned again. My brother put it back in the basement where he found it, and it may be there still.

This snooping was something my brother had learned from my father. Dad often searched our dresser drawers and book bags and listened in on phone extensions. His surveillance extended beyond his children, too. He worked as a switching technician at the phone company and occasionally he was called in to fix a problem with the electrical circuits on the weekend. I sometimes went with him as a young child, and a few times, he showed me a neat trick. In those days, floor to ceiling circuitry panels sat in rows like library stacks to handle the area's calls. The phone lines ran through the office, and were arranged within those panels according to a system he had memorized. He could connect a receiver at a certain spot and hear every word being said on that phone line.

On one of those occasions, he listened in on my mother's conversation with her sister. I stood only about waist high to him then, and when I recognized the voices, I looked up at him in surprise. He quickly disconnected, but not before I realized he'd done this often before, and sensed from his haste that he knew he shouldn't.

"Don't tell anybody about that," he said.

You never know who might read what you write, but you must also beware of who might overhear when you speak.

I don't know why Kitty had the letter that Clara had written to Lizzie, but I could easily see William discovering it while rifling through his wife's belongings as she hung out the wash or milked the cow—not because he had reason to suspect her of anything, but just because a man should know what goes on in his own house, even inside the heads of those who live there.

But perhaps I'm being unfair to my great-grandfather, whom I never met. If I give him the benefit of the doubt, I can imagine he found the letter after Kitty died, twenty years after they married and five years before his own death. The bittersweet chore of sorting through his loved one's belongings might have been punctuated by the discovery of a cache of letters, yellowed, folded, brittle at the seams, in faded cursive writing with varying degrees of legibility.

Perhaps I am completely wrong to attribute these tender motives for preserving letters to William. Perhaps he never found them, never read a one. They may all have lain forgotten in the backs of drawers until both Kitty and William had died, leaving my grandfather to do the keeping.

Today, Kitty and Lizzie would have chatted by phone or text, but in their era, before telephones were common, mother and daughter maintained their bond through the mail and occasional visits.

July 22, 1924

Dear Mother,

Will write you a few lines. Got home Sunday night before dark. It was raining when I got here and I had eat so many Collards I was sick when I did get home, but I sure did enjoy my supper. Well I sure hope you are feeling better by now. I had a letter from Walter and Clara last night and said they was getting along fine. Said they had a big family now the cat had five kittens.

I will send you those needles today. I was sick yesterday, but I feel better today and will go down the street and get them and mail them. Well I don't know anything to write only I hope you soon make up your mind to come up here for I want to see brother Clyde and I would like for you to come up here and he will be here, too, and we could go over to Winston-Salem with him and spend a night or two. Well I will close with lots of love, as ever your loving Daughter,

Elizabeth

Intimacy exists in a thousand shared trivial experiences that mortar together life's sporadic meaningful moments. As we would expect, some of Lizzie's letters record routine events, but others express a desperate need for her mother's presence.

Charlotte, N.C.
June 22, 1925

Dear Mother,

Will write you a few lines. I am sick and it looks like I can't get any better, so I am going somewhere or to the Hospital, I don't know which one, and I want you to come up here. Now listen, Ma, I want you to come right now. I am sending you the money, so don't disappoint me. Clyde is coming to go with me. Now be sure and catch the next train after you get this for I must see you right now. Well I am too sick to write any more, but catch the train. Will close and look for you Wednesday and if you don't come Wednesday, I will look for you not later than Thursday.

Don't write, come!

Lizzie

I can't get to the post office to Register this, but I guess you will get it alright.

Correspondence

Lizzie longs for her mother to comfort her in her illness, and she seems to childishly exaggerate her condition to strengthen her appeal. No other details remain about Lizzie's ailment or recovery or whether her mother rode the train to see her this time, but she did recover and continue to write.

> *Dear Mother,*
>
> *Got your letter today. Sure was glad to hear from you all. This leaves me feeling fine and hope you are the same. We was going to Columbia this week but it rained and snowed so I guess the roads are bad and we will wait until another time. I need the money anyway for other things. I am going to finish paying Mr. Windle today, then I may be able to get us some clothes. I hope so anyway. I thought I was going to get a little help but I see I didn't, so you know I don't beg no one to do anything for me. Well I don't know anything else to write so I guess I will close and wash some dishes and scrub the floor. Answer real soon.*
>
> *Lizzie*

Are the last few lines a passive-aggressive reproach against Kitty for not sending money? If her mother was not the disappointing party, the letter suggests that Kitty knew who was.

Around 1930, however, Lizzie's letters shift in tone. As she becomes aware of the strained relationship between her mother and her stepfather, she transforms from a supplicant to a shield.

Sunday afternoon

Dear Mother,

> *Got your letter yesterday and sure was glad to hear from you, but I sure have been worried about what you said about your Breakfast. I started to come down there this morning but I thought I would wait and come after you. Listen Ma, let me know what morning you can come and be ready early and I will come get you.*

This letter, though cryptic, is the first indication of conflict at Kitty's home. What happened at breakfast? Something that worried Lizzie enough to want to fetch her mother. I imagine a domestic tantrum, with William angry about something burnt, something undercooked, something late, or about something altogether unrelated that found its focus at the breakfast table. Perhaps he had rolled over to her in bed before dawn, sour breath in her face, fumbling with the fly of his briefs with one hand while hiking up her nightgown with the other. I imagine her pulling the hem of her gown while sliding from the bed. "Breakfast," she said. "The boys."

Of course, I will never know exactly what happened, but even if what I imagine is true, Kitty wouldn't be the first or last woman who needed to tread carefully around a temperamental man, a man whose ego was easily bruised by some neglected minor office or some unintentional show of willfulness.

My mother, for example, learned to pacify my father through selective silence and acquiescence. Like my father, she had been quite good looking when they married. She smiles out of old photos like a glamorous movie star of the late forties or early fifties, with stylish, short, dark hair, painted lips, high heels, and an almost-hour-glass figure. As it does with everyone, time has taken its toll on her face and figure. Now in her early eighties, she has lost the middle-aged spread that accumulated when I was a child, but her curves have flattened, her hair has whitened, and rheumatoid arthritis now twists and enlarges her knuckles. When I visited my parents a year or two after I received the box of letters, Mom complained to me with annoyance that my father had lately taken to supervising her in the kitchen, the one place where she had always been in charge, and interfering with her usual methods. He would take the bread and toaster to the screened back porch, for example, so the heat wouldn't hamper the kitchen's air conditioning. Sitting on a wooden chair near the outlet, he'd brown a plateful of toast and then bring it back to the kitchen for her to make sandwiches.

"He's just slowing me down," she grumbled.

"Why don't you tell him to stop?"

"Oh, you know, I just like to keep the peace," she sighed. "We're both too old to change now."

Apparently, Kitty was not so willing to efface herself in the name of peacekeeping. Lizzie's next letter to Kitty seems more desperate than the previous one, and suggests that she feared for her mother's physical safety.

Wednesday Morning

Dear Mother,

Received your letter this morning and sure was sorry to hear about your troubles. Now listen, why don't you come on home where you belong. You know if you would you can have anything you want and then I would not be worried to death all the time. And then when your people come to see you they would not be any one to get mad about it. Now listen, sell your cow for just what you can get for her and put your clothes in your trunk and wire me and I will come get you or I'll send the money and let you come on the train. Just anything suits you I will do. You know you have three homes as long as you have three children. Now listen Ma, let me know by Saturday morning what you are going to do, for if you are not coming I am going to Clyde's Saturday evening, but unless I hear from you I will be so worried I can't enjoy myself. So write me or wire me if you are coming and I will mail you the money or come for you, either one. Am fixing to eat

*dinner and have fried chicken. Sure wished you was
here right now and help me eat it. Lots of love, Lizzie.*
(Oh, yes, two times)
*Ma, I have got a good mind to come down
there and not wait to see what you say. I guess it
would be best to wait for if I come I will bring you
back if you wanted to come or if you don't want to
come. I may do that anyway for the more I write the
madder I get. Send me a Special Delivery so I can
get it at once. I guess I better stop for I am about as
mad as I can get. Here is stamps for a Special so put
them on it.*

Even family visits angered William. Yet Lizzie also
exhibited a proprietary attitude over her mother, going so far
as to urge her to leave her husband. Lizzie and William each
seemed threatened by the other's claim to Kitty's affections.

I now believe my father and I fought a similar battle over
my mother's loyalties, if not her affection. Each of us craved
control over the household for which she, as its caretaker and
almost constant occupant, was the symbol.

As a young teenager, I shared and stoked my mother's
frustrations at my father's autocracy, and like Lizzie, I
encouraged her to leave her husband. Like a cancer, my hatred
for my father metastasized when he beat me with a leather
belt because I had disobeyed him and walked a friend home
from church. Belt-shaped bruises and welts covered my hips,
back, and thighs, and I seethed with impotent rage for years
afterward.

"We could get an apartment," I reasoned to my mother.

"And pay for it with what?" She hadn't worked outside the home in over twenty years. Her name wasn't even on the checking account until I was in middle school. But leaving was a constant fantasy, and my mind repeatedly wrestled with the puzzle of how. Today, in my fifties, I still have dreams in which I can't move out of my parents' house because I've lost the address of the apartment I paid down on. I spend my dream energy exploring new techniques for finding the place.

Back then, the practical barriers to leaving didn't stop me from pointing out domestic injustices at every turn, such as when Dad bought a .22 rifle for himself but vetoed Mom's new curtains as a waste of money. At fifteen, a few years into this war, I believed that I was winning ground when I overheard a conversation between my parents. I stood in the den next to their bedroom, halted by the sound of my name and the frustration in my father's voice.

"She's trying to turn everyone in the house against me," my father said. He was right, and my ego swelled with the knowledge that he found my influence threatening. Despite my efforts and minor successes, though, I never won the battle; Mom never openly sided with me against my father, but I didn't stop trying until long after I'd grown up and moved away from home.

Not until I was a middle-aged woman did I realize that this resentment that I guarded and fed did far more harm to me than it ever did to my father. I partially attribute my series of failed marriages to this emotional cathexis I created as a child, to that toxic fury that seared me from the inside, that I was too young to satisfy and too stubborn to abandon. My father's love was strong, stifling, and full of his own deeply-embedded insecurities; mine, in each of my failed adult relationships, swung from this extreme to a detachment as steady as a paid assassin's. And many times in my adult life, I've acted out that frustrated fantasy of escape that I couldn't push my mother toward.

Like me, Lizzie fails in her early attempts to repossess her mother, but William does not appear to have complete control of Kitty, either. Kitty's next letter to Lizzie calms the daughter's fears while explaining the anger that provoked them.

Blythewood, SC
Sept. 6 - 30

Dear Lizzie,

Just a few lines to let you know I am feeling fine. Sure hope this will find you well and feeling good. I hope you will have a good time at Clyde. Wish I could go with you. Maybe next time you all go out to the farm I will be there to go with you. Lizzie, don't be worrying yourself about me at all. I'm alright. He just got mad because I went out to Rose and eat Supper, but that's not going to stop me from going to Rose's. I will go again next time and eat, too. The cow's not keeping me here at all. Whenever I get ready to come, Warren can milk. If

you get sick or anything let me know. I will come.
Well, be good and let me hear from you soon.
    Love your Mother,

Kitty

Rose was Kitty's sister, who lived about twenty miles away in Columbia, and Warren was William's youngest son, about fourteen at the time of this letter. Kitty does not choose to leave, as Lizzie asked her to, and she does not pledge to "keep the peace," as my mother did. Instead, she says that she will stand and fight her battle at home. I am fascinated by the mention of the cow in these two letters. Obviously, the cow's milk would have been nurturing for the family, and it must have belonged to Kitty because Lizzie urged her to sell it before coming to Charlotte. But if the cow was not keeping her there, what was? I wonder if it was love.

Soon, though, Kitty's duty to her own children pulled her away from William temporarily.

Monday Morning

Dear Will,

Just a few lines to let you know I got here alright and found Clyde in the Hospital in a cast from his shoulders to his hips. No one knows how

long he will have to stay. The Dr. don't even know.
He had fell and hurt his back bad, but Lizzie knew
I would worry so that's why she didn't tell me. You
all let me know how the Baby is if she is better. The
reason Clyde is here is headquarters for the Tel
Co. The Company Dr. stays here and they bring
every body that gets hurt in South Carolina, North
Carolina, and Georgia. They have a man up here
from Columbia with his arm broke. Well it's time for
the mail and we have got to get ready to go to the
Hospital, so write at once.

Kitty

After her son Clyde recovered, Kitty returned to William, but the letters show that, true to her word, she continued to visit her family when she chose. And the tension with William continued as well. Throughout the rest of her life, letters summoned Kitty from Blythewood to Charlotte and back again, to care for her children or William. At one point, William's daughter-in-law, my grandmother, wrote on his behalf asking Kitty to come home, advising her that William was "worried to death" and wanted her "to come back real bad sure enough." Another time, his son Warren telegrammed Kitty, urging her to "COME AT ONCE PAPA IS SICK."

By contrast, my mother and father seldom leave the house separately these days. This togetherness might be a form of protection for two frail bodies that don't get around as well as they used to, and it might also be a sign of affection, or at least comfort, for two people who have grown so used to each other's company that they feel anxious when apart. It's at least in part a sign of possessiveness, though one that I don't believe my mother entirely welcomes. At times within the last ten years, I've invited my mother out to lunch or to go shopping, activities she once enjoyed; she declines, saying, "He doesn't like for me to go off without him." On the phone is the only time I can talk to her alone, and even then, I'm not always sure.

Yet, not too long ago, this self-sacrificing woman gave me one of the best pep talks I've ever had. This was about five years ago, shortly after my father gave me the box of letters.

I had called her on the phone, heartbroken. My fourth husband had left me for a younger woman, someone he knew from work.

"No," she said. "He left you for a woman with less education than you, who makes less money than you. He left you for a woman who makes him feel more important by comparison."

This was the treasure given by my mother, a gift for the present in contrast to my father's ones from the past. I have easily seen the similarities between William Warren and my father, but my mother's words remind me of the fight I see in Kitty—or, at least, they strengthen the fighter in me. As my mother and I grow older, I wish I'd known she had that wisdom within her sooner, and that I'd had opportunities to experience it more often.

Finally, though, the tug-of-war with Kitty took its toll. On a last visit to Lizzie in 1944, Kitty passed away from acute endocarditis, an infection of the heart lining. I imagine the worry that would have plagued William when he received a letter informing him of her illness, which was probably mistaken for the flu until it was too late. His greatest fear, losing her to her relatives, was realized.

This time, William saved a newspaper obituary documenting his wife's death. She was buried with the other Whitmans at Sandy Level Baptist Church in Blythewood. What the newspaper doesn't reveal, however, is that the rivalry over Kitty didn't end with her death. Within a year, Lizzie summoned her mother home again, exhuming her body to be reburied next to her first husband in Charlotte. She erected a large headstone bearing a clear portrait of Kitty at about age sixty above her name and dates. Below these, she had engraved the statement, "Mother is not dead. She is only sleeping." William, nearly seventy, let Kitty go.

But he kept her letters. He kept them in his family to preserve a part of Kitty, keeping her words as an act of love, love that he had never fully differentiated from control.

Just days ago, I spoke to my father on the phone to ask some more questions about Kitty and William, but he had already told me what he knew, and now the details are getting harder for him to remember. I also asked if he had received an essay I'd mailed to him, one I'd recently published in a magazine.

"Yeah, we read it," he said. "It's in there on the dresser now with another one you wrote." Then, proudly, "I've saved all the writing you've ever sent me."

— 3 —

The Cup

It is only our heartbreak that refutes
all that is ephemeral in love.

—Amor Towles, *A Gentleman in Moscow*

At four feet and eleven inches, my great-aunt Ella was almost as round as she was tall. Her short black-and-gray hair and wide face perched atop a shapeless cotton dress, knee-high stockings, and flat loafers. On a summer afternoon, she sat on our front porch drinking a glass of iced tea and relishing the details of the story she told my mother.

"Thought it was dead. In the country, they didn't always have a doctor come back then, and the funerals happened quicker. They were droppin' the casket down when the baby started cryin'." She rocked in her chair and shifted her glass in her hands, wiping its cool condensation on her brow. Her feet rested flat on the porch's terracotta tiles, and her stomach rested contentedly on her thighs; her dress modestly covered her comfortably spread knees. "They pulled it up quick, the mama screamin' and carryin' on. But it died shortly anyway. Had to have the funeral all over ag'in."

Mama did not react to this story, in my opinion at age seven, with the appropriate shock and horror.

"Wait—what?" I wanted to ask, forgetting about the mosquito bite I had been scratching behind my knee. "Whose baby? How did they not know? What was wrong with it?" But I knew if I asked, my mother would send me off to play, so I listened quietly and hoped that more would be revealed.

It wasn't. My mother shifted the conversation to other topics. Years later, when I asked Mama about this story, she didn't remember it. She doubted it really happened, but not that Aunt Ella said it did. Apparently, Aunt Ella liked to "tell stories," which, in my mother's family's vocabulary, was a euphemism for lying. When I was about twelve, my cousin Tammy, just a year older than me, was the first to inform me that Ella had a story of her own. Ella lived with her sister Louise in a small house a few blocks from mine. She had an adult son named Dale, with a wife and kids an hour or so away.

In one of our many after-school phone conversations, Tammy asked me if I'd ever wondered where Aunt Ella's husband, Dale's father, was. I hadn't.

"I guess he died or they got divorced," I offered, lying on my neatly-made bed and watching the dust motes dance in the afternoon light. I held the phone with one hand and idly twisted its spiraled cord around the other.

"But a woman is supposed to change her name when she gets married. So, why are Dale and Aunt Ella's last names the same as her sister's?"

I hadn't wondered this either, but of course, Tammy already knew the answers to the questions she asked. In this way, I learned that Ella had never married. Unwed mothers were something of a scandal in the late-1920s South Carolina into which Dale was born, and apparently still were to my cousin and me in 1980. I hung up the phone and left my bedroom seeking confirmation for these revelations. My mother, cutting out a dress pattern at the kitchen table, wouldn't talk much except to acknowledge that what we suspected was true. I don't remember her exact words, but her tone contained a reprimand, possibly for delving into topics she considered too mature for us or for besmirching Ella's present-day reputation. When I was older and still curious, she told me more.

It is hard for me to imagine the old woman I grew up around attracting the sexual attention of men. But in a black-and-white picture of Ella as a young adult, she wears a stylish bob, holds her head at a saucy angle, and appears ready to laugh out loud; she seems a little daring and probably a lot of fun. In that photo, her plump figure rounding out her dress suggests candor and plenty rather than dowdiness. A sassy and stubborn girl, Ella was happy to take shortcuts and quick to speak her mind, but because she was born poor in Columbia, South Carolina, in 1909, these character traits were especially unfavorable.

When her father died in 1917, her mother was unable to pay the rent. She moved the family in with her brother, making a household of fifteen souls. Never fond of the tedium and toil of school, Ella gladly quit after sixth grade, but soon realized the work at home was harder than any she'd done in the classroom. She reluctantly learned to cook, clean, and care for the younger children while the adults and older children labored on her uncle's farm. Her mother remarried almost a decade later. Their material circumstances improved, but I imagine Ella bridled at this strict new father figure imposed on her late teenage years.

She liked to walk to neighbors' houses or to catch a ride to Main Street for window shopping. Sometimes boys would visit the house, and she'd dash up the stairs, begging a sibling to bring up water for washing while she quickly brushed her hair. After cleaning up, she'd casually walk downstairs and spend an hour or so flirting with the boy on the front porch, threatening younger siblings who violated their privacy. A swimming hole, Moe's Pond, was also a favorite destination of teens in summer months, and Ella went if she could talk one of her older sisters into going along.

But the most popular outing in Ella's day was the church social, where teens and unmarried young adults gathered to talk, eat, sing, play charades or tug-of-war, and flirt under the watchful eyes of married couples in good standing. Recently, my mother told the story of one social where Ella, then about sixteen, met a young man who found her lively personality enticing. At the end of the evening, this young man offered to walk her home. For several blocks, they gossiped about the people they'd seen, and Ella basked in his attention.

At her house, she invited him in to meet her large family, among them her eighteen-year-old sister, my future grandmother. In contrast to Ella's bubbly fullness, my young grandmother was statuesque, aloof, and dignified. She hadn't gone to the social because she found the games and the company tiresome. When this young man saw my grandmother, my mother tells me, it was something close to love at first sight. Within days, he called on her again, and within months they married.

Now, Ella barely knew this young man at the time, but it had to have wounded her pride when, after walking her home, my future grandfather chose her sister over her. Adding insult to injury, her sister's wedding happened on the heels of her mother's, and they all moved together to a small, rented farm in the Dutch Fork community just outside of Columbia. The older couple farmed, and my grandfather landed a job hauling dirt for the new man-made lake and hydro-electric dam being constructed in 1927. By the time Ella turned nineteen, however, she rebelled against the tedium and isolation of country living, where her only activities were farming, keeping house, and tending to younger children. Ella longed for excitement, or at least distraction. Her eventual plan was to marry like her sister, but she intended to have fun in the meantime. So, after fights and sullen protests, her mother and stepfather agreed to her temporary move into the home of her Aunt Suzy, back in Columbia, where she could find a job and send money home to the family.

About this time, she met Wilbur Donnelly, a former farm laborer in his early twenties who liked drinking, gambling, and Ella. What did she see in him? Maybe he was a way out, a stop-block to prevent her eventual return to the farm, where she would have a front-row seat to the honeymoon phase of her sister's marriage. Maybe she felt that the chores and rules at her mother's house were too oppressive for an almost-grown woman who had helped run the household since she was ten years old.

On the other hand, maybe Wilbur swept Ella off her feet. I picture him with a sexy swagger, like Marlon Brando in The Wild One, minus the motorcycle. Manly, irreverent, and defiant, he was just bad enough to be good, and she gulped down the attention he poured over her. For him, a job was necessary only to finance his fun, and he always had more fun with company, particularly lively, attractive company like Ella. With him, she could experience the freedom she had always wanted but had been taught was wrong: staying out almost every night, sometimes to the early morning; government-banned alcohol; sex, of course; laughing loud and often; but mostly just relaxing the edges of her personality, letting the border of her self rest where it fell naturally, rather than sucking it in to fit the mold made for her by her family.

She found in Wilbur her reason to thrust off her restrictive training wholesale, without taking time herself to sort the good from the bad. I'm sure it didn't take much game to win the heart of a young, poor, and ignorant girl. I'm also sure he promised to marry her, as soon as he got a better job, as soon as he had enough money saved, as soon as… He may have meant it, too.

Regardless of the reasons, Ella humiliated her family by abandoning Aunt Suzy's house to live with Wilbur. Their son Dale was born in July 1929.

When Ella went into labor, family legend has it, Wilbur sat on the porch drinking with his friends. Ella's mother, present to witness her daughter's shame and, if possible, to bring life into the world without her daughter leaving it, had to run them out. I picture the men wearing shabby fedoras and rolled shirtsleeves, sitting in tilted chairs on the worn, unpainted boards of the rented house's porch, smoking and laughing, a little drunk, with glasses of brown liquor in their hands, and a half-empty, unlabeled bottle perched on the railing, filtering the summer evening sun.

Here I imagine Wilbur as Henry Fonda's Tom Joad rather than Brando's Johnny Strabler. He's a little beaten down, but still rough and sexy. He's nervous about his child's impending birth, but can't express this in a conventional way. Ella's mother, a stout lady with her hair in a bun and her arms folded on her chest, marches through the screen door, letting it slap shut behind her.

"This is no place for you men to be drinking," she orders, and shoos them down the road.

With her mother's help, Ella delivered the baby in her bed.

A 1930 census document shows Ella and Wilbur living together as husband and wife in Columbia, near the textile mill where Ella later worked for most of her life, but they never actually had the benefit of a clergy. They shared the mill house with another couple, ages eighteen and fifteen, also listed as married. It must have been soon after 1930 that Ella and Wilbur's relationship ended.

Perhaps he wearied of her and the baby, or perhaps he met another woman and decided to move on. As the mother of an infant, Ella couldn't share in the late-night merriment as often as she used to, and I imagine Wilbur went on without her. Maybe he found another girl, a wild girl not yet disfigured by pregnancy and childbirth, not yet burdened by a baby, whose body had not yet become so numbingly familiar to him. Men are often guilty of such treachery in books and movies. After having taken everything from her, he moved on to his next conquest. "When Lovely Woman Stoops to Folly," a famous eighteenth-century poem that was still popular in Ella's day, suggests that a woman's only recourse after such a tragedy of her own making is to die, but Ella, of course, survived.

Ella's life was no poem, book, or movie, so perhaps the relationship ended differently. The carefree lover soon became the deadbeat. His liquor-drinking used scant resources that were needed to feed their baby, and, of course, she couldn't work while caring for an infant. The support of family and friends was tentative at best, and Ella worried about her child's future. She pleaded and gave ultimatums, but Wilbur remained raucous as ever. Then, when he stayed away all night and into the next morning, leaving nothing but dry flour in the house, she made her decision.

Whether he left her or she left him, Wilbur was never a part of his son's life after that. After the breakup, thanks to the intervention of my grandparents, Ella and Dale moved back in with Ella's mother and stepfather, who had recently returned to Columbia.

"This is our place, too," my grandfather told her morally outraged stepfather. "If Ella and the baby can't stay here, we'll move out and get us another place where they're welcome."

So they stayed. My grandmother was having babies of her own by then, and she took care of Dale while Ella went to work in the spinning room of the Olympia Textile Mill.

Lucky to get a job at all in the depressed economy, she worked second shift, 2 p.m. to 11 p.m., for little pay. At the mill, she gossiped with the other women, coolly flirted with the men, and avoided what labor she could. She didn't like the long hours, and the night shift workers scared each other with rumors of the mill's ghost, a boy who had been worked to death by the company owner and disposed of in the mill's giant furnace. Union organizers used the ghastly tales to stir up hatred for the bosses, but for Ella, these stories were just to pass the time and didn't offer enough incentive to risk losing her job by joining a union.

Then, when Ella's son was about ten years old, she met a man named Morris, who loved her and seemed to love Dale, too. "I'll take care of you both," he said.

They planned to marry, and he frequently visited the family's house to court her. No one had much money, so most Saturday afternoons were spent eating ice cream or watermelon on the porch with Ella's relatives while the children played in the yard. On one of these occasions, my grandfather, who had a playful streak, began to tease his prospective brother-in-law.

"What are you gonna do with Dale when he gets older, Morris? Ella won't let nobody else lay a hand on him. One day, he's gonna whip you!"

Apparently a man who easily took offense, Morris felt his manhood was being challenged. "I'll whip Dale if he gets outta line," he said, "and Ella, too, if she needs it!"

My grandfather laughed and smoothed things over, and the pleasant afternoon resumed, but Ella began to worry how this man would treat her son, now a rowdy and mischievous boy on whom she doted. She broke the engagement, and her love life ended there.

I don't believe she did this lightly. Morris's comment likely confirmed doubts that had weighed on Ella's mind for some time. Maybe she'd witnessed his temper seethe when they were alone and feared that, once he was sure of her, it would erupt to punish her and her son for being the best that Morris could do.

She had to have been heartbroken at the loss of love, or at least at the loss of marriage. Now heavier, nearly thirty, with a bastard child, Ella had to have foreseen the countless partnerless days ahead and the lifetime of partial dependency on married relatives. If she felt shame at her condition, she had to have mourned this lost chance to live it down.

I wonder if she shielded her son from this grief or if she relied on him as a buttress. I know how tempting it must have been to transform her son from an innocent bystander to an ally and a balm. No doubt she knew that she should preserve his worry-free childhood as long as possible, put on a face that hid her despair and confusion at how she had gotten to this place, but she also believed it would lessen her pain to share it with the one person who had been closest to her during that ill-fated relationship.

As my fourth marriage ended, I longed to cling to my seven-year-old son like a life raft, but I also knew that my grief had the potential to swamp him. Some days I did fine, but I am ashamed to say that, other days, especially in the beginning, I did not. I had an older child from a previous marriage, whose gender and relative maturity would have made them a slightly more appropriate source of solace, but still, I wished for an ally in this boy whose father, I believed, had wronged me.

I remember the day after Memorial Day, just a week after I discovered the girlfriend my soon-to-be-ex had had for months. I sat on the couch next to my blond-haired, blue-eyed child as he explained a new game he'd learned to play on my laptop. Unable to focus on his chatter, I blurted, "Your dad went to a pool party on Sunday with his new girlfriend."

I wanted this little boy to comfort me, to share my anger and jealousy, although I knew that, for him, it would be about the missed pool party and not about the other woman. In response, my round-faced child, already learning to protect himself from my pain, looked me in the eye with a deep but controlled sorrow. His lip barely trembled as he said, "Please don't make me sad today. I just want to have a good day."

Dale would have been a bit older than my boy, a little less vulnerable and a little more tainted by experience, so it would have been easier for Ella to burden him with her heartache. But I imagine Aunt Ella to be a stronger woman, of necessity, who stoically shut her tears in a box and buried them so no one would see.

Having Dale made Ella's life more difficult, and, as a bastard, Dale didn't exactly have it easy. When he joined the army at eighteen, confusion arose when the name on his birth certificate didn't match the name he'd always gone by, and the circumstances of his birth became common knowledge among his comrades. Dale spent his whole life fighting in one way or another: against those who sneered at his origins, against his own lack of self-esteem.

I usually saw Dale only once a year, at the family Christmas Eve party, and I remember him as a middle-aged man with male pattern baldness, a paunch, horn-rimmed glasses, and a perpetual cigarette dangling from his lip. We called him Uncle Dale because he was about our parents' age, but he was really my second cousin. He was always drunk at these parties, and

I remember hearing his wife say, "Just once, I wish he would wait to start drinking until we got here."

The year I was thirteen, I decided to sneak some liquor for myself, quick splashes of bourbon in my Coke when no one was watching, and soon I was drunk. I sat on an upholstered ottoman in the den, then slid off it to the floor, laughing as my purple skirt slipped up to nearly my waist. Uncle Dale plopped down on the floor in front of me. "Well, goddamn!" he said, also laughing. Yes, I thought. Precisely.

After many years of hard drinking, Dale died before his mother did, at about age fifty, of liver cancer. Aunt Ella had retired from the mill and now lived alone in a house a few blocks up the hill from mine, her housemate and sister Louise also having died of cancer. I can't recall that I ever saw Dale talking much with his mother, and I never talked to her about how it felt to lose her only child. But after his death, she seemed withered by sorrow, like a human husk that continued to talk and eat and move, but without pleasure.

My parents saw Aunt Ella's experiences as a life lesson for me. Like the young Ella, I, too, was freer with boys than was wise, and like her son Dale, I enjoyed the taste of alcohol more than was healthy. The spring after the Christmas party, for example, my first boyfriend, a sweet and skinny star drummer in the middle school band, showed up at the bus stop with a fifth of Bacardi he'd stolen from home.

I had been the chubby kid throughout elementary school, frequently teased by others who appeared effortlessly thin. I once fought with my older brother, who, seeing me doing toe touches in my bedroom, taunted, "Do it, Fats!" At nine, I still played with Barbie Dolls, mainly because I idolized their image of female beauty. I recall falling asleep with Barbie's figure in my head—naked, plastic breasts swelling perfectly above her tiny waist and long, shapely-thin, elegant legs—and a prayer on my lips that I would wake to look like her. With the onset of puberty, I metamorphosed from my cocoon shape, not into a Barbie Doll, but into a willowy adolescent, and the novel attentions of boys enthralled me.

My first boyfriend's straight, dirty-blond hair hung over his forehead and past his ears, and he laughed joyfully and easily. I remember his tanned skin, rounded nose, and deep brown eyes. It didn't take much to convince me to skip school that day. I had recently decided that, if I could receive such brutal punishment for something as innocent as walking a friend home from church, I might as well do whatever I wanted and damn the consequences. After all, they couldn't kill me, I reasoned.

As the school bus approached, we ducked behind a parked car. Then we walked to a popular spot in the nearby woods where bushes and briars formed a natural cave, and drank by turns straight from the bottle, pausing between swigs to make out. The rum burned as it went down, and my eyes watered, but I doggedly kept at it as if it were a sacred duty. A little later, we stumbled to the neighborhood park, climbed inside the playground fort made from wood and old tires, and made out some more.

Eventually, we connected with another friend who hadn't gone to school that day (she lived with her grandmother, who worked during the day, and she hardly ever went to school that year), finished the liquor, smoked some weed at the park, and bought potato chips and Twinkies at the convenience store.

At the end of the school day, I walked home on schedule. But, of course, I reeked of alcohol. It oozed from my pores and probably had baptized my clothes as I drank it. Although I didn't have enough experience to realize it, I'm sure I was still drunk.

I had hoped that I could avoid Mom well enough to hide what I'd been doing all day, and that when Dad got home from work, all residual effects would have worn off. I was actually surprised when Mom accused me of drinking.

"How did she know?" I asked my older sister when my mother was out of earshot.

"You stink!" my older sister announced. "She can smell it across the room."

My mother called the school and learned that I hadn't attended that day. I was lucky that my mother was the only parent home at the time and that she was so angry she whipped me. My parents had a type of double-jeopardy rule. If one parent beat us, the other one wouldn't do it again for the same offense.

She had me bend over her bed and retrieved one of my dad's extra belts from the closet.

"How could you do such a thing at a time like this?" she asked, punctuating her question with a blow. Aunt Louise, Ella's sister, was in the hospital at the time, dying of pancreatic cancer, and my mother had been there most of the day visiting. Shamefully, I felt only a twinge of guilt.

Mostly I felt grateful. Mom simply wasn't as strong as Dad, and while her whacks with the belt stung through my jeans, they weren't hard enough to leave bruises.

This time, however, my dad created a work-around for their "no-double-whipping" rule. The next day he took me to the basement, to my older brother's bedroom, and had me lean over the bed and prop myself up with my arms. He took his belt off and informed me that he was going to have a talk with me.

"But if you relax your arms or drop your weight down on the bed, I'm going to whip you," he said in the dank, windowless room.

An interrogation and shaming about the previous day followed. I guess he was counting on me being hungover and frightened, but I stayed calm and my arms remained strong for what must have been thirty minutes. Even at the time, I thought this episode was creepy, sadistic, and just plain odd, but he didn't end up beating me, and I suppose there's integrity in that.

I was suspended for the last week of seventh grade and grounded for the entire summer. My mother and father switched me to a different public school in a better neighborhood, away from the bad influences of my boyfriend and friends. I didn't see that sweet drummer again until the summer after high school graduation, when he stopped by my parents' house one afternoon. At the time, I was watching TV in the den with my future first husband, and my mother answered the front door.

She walked back to the den to say I had a visitor, and to my boyfriend she said slyly, "Don't worry, he's riding a bike."

He looked almost the same, still sweet and happy, and we had an awkward ten-minute chat before he mounted his bike and rode away. I later learned that he died of cancer at age thirty-five.

Today I know that the school transfer was the right move, but at the time, I grew angrier, lonelier, and more determined to find new bad influences.

It didn't take long.

I first laid eyes on Kevin exiting the science classroom as I entered it between periods. At my old school, most of the kids looked like understudies for the Ramones. At the new school, they could have been understudies for the cast of *Pretty in Pink*. Boys and girls wore Izod or Ralph Lauren shirts in pastels and jewel tones. On cooler days, they donned Members Only jackets or down ski vests, and in rainy weather, L. L. Bean duck shoes. For both genders, hair was often feathered, but long hair was strictly reserved for girls, who employed hot rollers in their style regimen.

At sixteen, Kevin stood at least a head taller than the sea of eighth-grade boys. He'd just moved to South Carolina from California, he said, with his mother and brothers. He'd been held back twice.

Dark-brown hair hung down to his shoulders and into his face, until he flipped it aside, revealing London-blue eyes beneath bushy eyebrows. He wore a leather bomber jacket with a faux fur collar over his faded jeans and t-shirt. When I imagine Ella seeing Wilbur for the first time, this is what I picture. I looked forward to the five minutes before science class every day, resolved to make him notice me.

Through my sheer persistence, he eventually became my acquaintance and then my boyfriend. Because my parents were so strict, our interactions consisted mostly of sitting together on the playground at lunchtime, a few stealthy kisses, and occasional phone calls. I also routinely did his homework, which took me all of five minutes each night. It went on this way for a few months until Kevin grew bored.

"You're sweet and pretty," he said, "but I'm used to having sex with my girlfriends."

When he broke up with me, I mourned the loss of all he represented: coolness, rebellion, and my access to these things. I recognize this in hindsight, but at the time, I was just a heartbroken teenager rejected by the love of her life.

Before long, however, I saw an opportunity to win him back.

Just before spring break, a popular girl in the eighth grade was having a house party at the home of her older, married sister, who would chaperone. She invited me, and miraculously, I was allowed to go. I told Kevin I was going, and we began talking more and more at lunchtime in the days before the party until we came up with the plan that I would sneak off that night to meet him. We were back together.

I arrived at the party around 7 p.m. with the details in my head. After my father dropped me off, I would wait a few minutes and then walk about a half-mile on the dark neighborhood streets to meet Kevin at a gas station. He was babysitting for a married couple, and his brothers would give us a ride there and back.

The split-level ranch house sat on a slightly sloped, grass-covered lawn. I walked up the driveway to the brightly-lit, carless carport on the right rear, where most of the kids congregated. A classmate held a two-liter bottle of Coke and offered me some.

The Cup

"Taste it," he said.

I took a swig and discovered a generous dose of liquor mixed with the soda. At that moment, our chaperone poked her head out of the door, holding her baby, and said hello. Maybe twenty-five, she adopted the part of the cool but responsible adult role model, intent on being occasionally visible, but mostly staying out of the way.

"Thanks," I laughed to my classmate as she ducked back inside. The bottle made its rounds, and I glanced at the street to see that my father's yellow Pacer still stood sentry a few houses down. Throughout the rest of eighth grade, and occasionally in high school, this car would be known among my peers as "the stake-out car" because of what was to happen that night. Even when I began driving myself to school in the spring of tenth grade, my pride in my new freedom diminished when a mean-spirited boy asked, "Isn't that the stake-out car?"

"Why is he still here?" I asked myself, but I knew the answer: he sat in the dark car watching the house through the rear-view mirror, making sure I stayed put.

If he didn't leave soon, I would miss my rendezvous with Kevin. My plan would be foiled. Thoughts racing, pulse quickening, and chest tightening, I couldn't stand still. Another child might have interpreted this circumstance as a sign that the universe intended her to scrap the scheme and enjoy the party with her peers. At the time, I would have said this meeting mattered so much because of my love for Kevin. But now I'm sure that at least part of its importance was related to asserting my right to define myself, however ill-advised that might be.

As a parent of teenagers now, I am daily thankful that mine are not as bad as I was, and among the conflicted feelings I now have for my own aging parents are shame and regret for my actions at this point in my life. Both of my children are smart, and my older one claims autonomy in a creative, dreamy landscape. A latent artist, this child usually dwells on a plane apart from typical adolescent drama, but they have lately seen the potential power in directing artistic vision at the world to fight injustice. My younger child couples his intelligence with the same willfulness that I felt at his age. We have clashed at times, and I have had to learn to let the small stuff go (strict bedtimes, regularly cleaning his room), and to speak and listen to him respectfully so he, in turn, will respect me enough to benefit from my experience regarding the big stuff.

On the night of the party, adrenaline fueled my problem-solving skills while manic defiance and determination suppressed my judgment. So, I enlisted the help of an accomplice, the closest one at hand.

"My dad hasn't left. He parked his car right down the street," I told the bottle boy.

"Really?" He walked down the driveway, looked to the left, and walked back. "That's weird. Is he going to sit out there all night?"

"I don't know, but I'm supposed to meet Kevin soon," I said, my voice anxious and exasperated. "He's waiting for me at the gas station, and if I don't leave in a few minutes, I'll miss him."

"I have a moped. I can give you a ride, if you want." I'm not sure why he offered to help me. I do remember his name, but we weren't really friends, and he certainly wasn't friends with Kevin. Too rough and dangerous for most of the kids at my school, Kevin hadn't been invited to this party.

I accepted the ride, and we climbed on his moped. He offered me his woven straw cowboy hat that he'd brought to the party as a novelty item, and I held it on, a makeshift disguise, as we sped out of the driveway and down the road—away from the stake-out car.

My classmate dropped me off across the street from the gas station where Kevin stood next to a small, dark-blue coupe, looking for me.

"I almost gave up on you," he said as I approached the car. "I didn't think you were coming."

"My dad wouldn't leave," I said vaguely. "I got a ride from a friend with a moped."

He introduced me to his two brothers, both of whom appeared to be somewhere around twenty, and cultivated the style (western hat, long hair, and beard) of Ronnie Van Zant, lead singer of Lynyrd Skynyrd, killed just four years earlier in a plane crash.

We dropped by the family apartment, where I met their mother. I remember thinking that she looked older than I had expected, with short graying hair, a middle-aged spread, and a weary, lined face. She looked at me skeptically, and her polite hello seemed like a small dam that held back doubts and questions she was too tired to raise. The news that I would be babysitting with Kevin brought no outward objection.

After a short visit, the brothers drove us over to the friends' townhouse in a nearby complex. We entered through a sliding glass door to the living room. From here, I saw an open dining room and kitchen, and a half bath to the side. Up the stairs were bedrooms and another bath. The couple had two children, a toddler, still awake, and a sleeping infant.

The husband, who looked a lot like Kevin's brothers, greeted us warmly. Unperturbed by my presence, he asked us to smoke with him while his wife finished getting ready upstairs. He sat on the sofa, lit a joint, and passed it to Kevin, who toked and passed it to me. I hadn't smoked in months, maybe once since moving to the new school, and I was relieved that my first drag of the acrid, skunky weed didn't provoke a coughing fit. In the picture of this night that still hangs in the gallery of my mind, I can't picture the toddler at that moment. Maybe he was upstairs with his mother; maybe he played quietly in the shadows.

Amidst the passing and smoking, the wife came downstairs. Like her husband, she was twenty-something. Her dark, straight hair hung to her mid-back; a blue-patterned polyester dress hugged her slim figure, and she wore too much eyeliner. Kevin introduced me to her, and she said hello but little else. The joint gone, the husband offered to fix us all a drink before they left, but I couldn't name a drink I'd like.

"How about a White Russian?" he suggested. "It tastes great. You'll like it."

We sipped our drinks, Kevin and the husband chatted casually, and although I wanted to belong in their world, I felt as out of place as a salamander in the Sahara Desert. I felt the wife eyeing me resentfully, probably wondering why I was in her home, wondering if she should leave her children. For some reason, she said nothing.

The Cup

Memory is strange. We create narratives from it that help us understand our experience, and sometimes we unconsciously change details to fit our script. Today I wonder why Kevin's mother or the mother of these small children didn't speak, but maybe I'm projecting silent objections onto them. Today, I wish one of them had derailed that train I had willingly boarded, with no intention of abandoning until it reached its destination.

"Well, have fun, and help yourself to whatever you like," the husband said as they departed for their date night. "I don't care what you do, as long as my kids aren't wandering around out in the dark when we get back."

As I recall the night, we got quickly down to business. Kevin settled the sleeping infant and the drowsy toddler on the sofa. He pulled heavy curtains across the sliding doors, turned off the light, and spread a blanket on the living room floor. From here, I remember still shots that flash across my memory like a faulty film flickering on the TV that played in the background.

✦ ✦ ✦

We are lying naked on the blanket. Kevin is touching me, and my skin feels numb and cold.

"Wait a minute," he says. He walks up the stairs, his naked back illuminated by the TV's ghostly light. He returns with Vaseline from the baby's room.

We recommence, and moments later, the toddler slides from the sofa and walks over to our heads on the carpet.

"Get back up there," Kevin says sternly. He rises and carries the toddler to the sofa, swatting his backside as he lays him down. "You stay there and go to sleep." He punctuates his words with a finger pointing in the child's face.

Returning to me on the blanket, he applies Vaseline and lies on top of me.

"You can make noise if you want to," he says into my ear. "It makes it better."

The first noise I make is in a frightened child's voice. "It hurts, it hurts!" I whine. For the first time, I want this to stop.

"Just a minute more. It'll stop hurting." And he is right. It does. Though the pain subsides, it is not replaced by pleasure, only pressure. I'm not sure how much time passes, and the only noise I'm aware of making is loud, ragged breathing.

✦ ✦ ✦

It ended with sudden knocking on the sliding glass doors a few feet to my left. We scrambled up, and Kevin handed me my clothes. I hurried to the half-bathroom to dress, and he let in his brothers, who had returned to take me back to the middle school party.

While I was in the bathroom, Kevin came to the door to hand me the panties that I had neglected in the rush to find clothes.

I could see in the mirror that my curly hair had formed an off-center helmet around my head, as if I had put it on crooked in the dark. Kevin smiled, shutting the door behind him, and smoothed my hair down.

"I'm proud of you," he said. "You did great. And I just let you enjoy it this time. I didn't cum, so you don't have to worry about getting pregnant."

One brother stayed with Kevin and the children, and the other drove me back to the party. He was polite and respectful, making small talk as I sat in the passenger seat of his car, but he knew exactly what we'd been doing.

"I'm going to let you off here," he said, stopping a few blocks away from the house. "I don't want any trouble."

As I walked the last few blocks in the dark, I wondered if I too could avoid trouble at this point. Maybe my father hadn't seen me leave. Could I slip back in unnoticed? Blocking panic, I sealed off my emotions and tried to channel my adrenaline into strategy. I imagined cutting through neighbors' yards and climbing fences, at the same time steeling myself for inevitable doom.

As I approached the party house in the cool night air, I saw that the yellow Pacer was gone, and my fear lifted momentarily. The milling kids under the carport lights ahead felt like a beacon.

I walked up the driveway, and the first kid I saw clued me in on the real situation.

"Tina, your dad has been here for hours looking for you. He's been yelling at everyone!" I took in his words but walked past without responding.

Under the carport, I saw the chaperone, still holding the now-sleeping baby. "Where did you go?! Your father's been here, and he's looking for you!"

"Where's my father?" I asked, looking past her, unable to focus on her words.

"The last time I saw him, he was out there," she said, nodding toward the front yard. "You don't know how much trouble you've caused tonight! Don't you ever do this to me again!"

For the first time, I made eye contact with her, thinking, "What a stupid thing to say. I don't even know you. I'm never even going to see you again. I have much bigger things to worry about right now." I didn't say anything, but my look must have conveyed some of this because her eyes softened. Most of the time at that age, and especially that night, I was incapable of appreciating the effect of my actions on others, whether due to adolescence, intoxication, or some more serious mental issue, I'm unsure.

At that moment, the stake-out car pulled into the driveway, and my dad jumped out and stalked toward me. To his barrage of questions about where I'd been and with whom, I responded honestly.

"You didn't walk all the way over there," the chaperone offered. Again, I looked at her blankly, this time thinking, "You don't belong in this conversation. You don't know him."

"Get in the car," my father said.

As we walked back down the driveway, I felt the eyes of the chaperone and the braver of my classmates watching us go. As we neared the car, my father grabbed a handful of my hair and shook hard enough to lift me off balance.

"You're just a little slut, aren't you!?" Then he let go, we got in the car, and we drove away.

In the weeks that followed, my parents' questions and accusations were intense, invasive, and intended to humiliate. With my dramatic teenage sensibility, I felt like a hostage enduring psychological torture. They might be able to control my physical freedoms at this point, but I determined that my psyche would be inviolable. I felt no shame at my actions; instead, I felt that I had proven to myself that I was desirable, and to my parents that I had some measure of independence. I know now that they wanted to protect me from myself, and if they had been different people, they might have sought the aid of family or child psychologists, but they were not that kind of people.

My lockdown for the rest of the school year was complete, and Kevin broke up with me again before the end of May. Everyone at the school seemed to know what had happened that night, either because Kevin had told them himself, or because the clues were all there from the night of the party. I was angry and deeply depressed, but I kept it hidden at school, a masking device that has proved useful later in life. I feigned ignorance of their knowledge, and confidence in myself, determined that my schoolmates would not define me either.

✦ ✦ ✦

By the summer after that party, Ella was a lonely old lady, and on a few steamy afternoons, I was sent up to her house to do penance for my teenage transgressions, my parents hoping I would see in her life a path I didn't want to trod.

I swept and vacuumed, listened to her talk about ailments and people I didn't know. So she wouldn't have to pay to get it done, I cut her already short, greasy hair as she sat on one of the white metal and plastic chairs of her dinette set. I wasn't trained to cut hair in any way, but my mother suggested that I do it. From Ella's harvest gold kitchen, I fetched the Little Debbies and Cokes that she wasn't supposed to have because of her type two diabetes. And at two and three p.m., we watched her "stories," *General Hospital* and *The Guiding Light*, in the sunroom off of the kitchen where the air-conditioning never worked well enough.

Our time together never went beyond feeling awkward to me, and perhaps to her as well. I did learn some lessons from her, but probably not the ones my parents had hoped. Inwardly, I rebelled against the injustice of all that had punished her: God, society, the times, her family, their narratives of the past. And deeper down, I learned a lesson I wouldn't appreciate until much later: that grief did not kill, at least not quickly.

After that summer, I didn't see Aunt Ella as often. She was older and frailer, and I was busy with school, work, other boyfriends. But when I got engaged to my first husband, as a freshman in college, a relative who didn't know me well dropped off a wedding gift at her house. My fiancé and I dutifully stopped in to visit and to open the gift in front of her. I had chosen a formal china pattern, delicate, white, and etched with small flowers along the edges. The three of us sat in her living room as I tore the silver paper from the box and carefully lifted the lid to find a white saucer and two halves of a white teacup inside.

"Now, I didn't do that," Ella said. "That box sat right there where they left it. I didn't do anything to it." Maybe I had looked at her in surprise when I saw the fractured china, but I hadn't thought she had broken it. Anyway, the box contained a gift receipt, and the cup could easily be exchanged for a whole one.

"I know," I tried to reassure her. "It probably got jostled when they were driving it over. This isn't the first time that's happened." But she continued peevishly denying any offense.

I left her house feeling discomfited. Was she growing senile, or had I unintentionally shot her an accusatory glance? Even if she had accidentally dropped the present, I wouldn't have been upset with her. Did her fervent denials expose her guilty conscience?

I know I saw Aunt Ella other times, but this is my last vivid memory of her. Several years after Dale died, after I had married for the first time and divorced two years later, Ella's grandson moved her down to a nursing home near his house in Charleston, where, I heard, she eventually lost both legs to diabetes-related complications. I didn't make it down to her funeral, soon thereafter, but I think about her still today.

Aunt Ella lived into her eighties, but she had lost so much along the way—her family's respect, Wilbur Donnelly, a second chance at love, her sister, her son, her home, even parts of her own body. She probably forgot about so trivial an accident as my broken wedding gift right after I left her house, but her initial reaction to it is what stays with me now. I opened the box to reveal something unexpectedly shattered within—an image that threatened to uncover her own held-in pain. Did that cracked china remind Aunt Ella of her many undeserved heartbreaks? Did her denials address imagined voices that declared that her pain had, in fact, been earned? Maybe beneath that lifted lid she saw what I could not: a warning of heartache for me.

— 4 —

Handling Shit and Finding Love

The women whom I love and admire for their strength and grace did not get that way because shit worked out. They got that way because shit went wrong, and they handled it. They handled it in a thousand different ways on a thousand different days, but they handled it.

—Elizabeth Gilbert, "Wisdom & Age & Women"

I respect people who handle "shit." The experience is never pleasant, for sure, but I admire those who handle life's messes stoically and continue on their paths.

At an early age, I learned that my maternal aunts could handle shit, literally. Great-Aunt Louise and Great-Aunt Ella both worked second shift at the Olympia Textile Mill, and when I was a child, they lived together in a small house a few blocks from my parents. While Aunt Ella was short and round, Louise was taller and thin. Whereas Aunt Ella talked and laughed easily, sometimes brashly, Aunt Louise was kind but dignified. Louise's black and gray hair formed stiff waves around her head, and her face, naturally dark from what my mother said was a splash of Native American blood, bore deep-set wrinkles and a leathery texture from lifelong smoking.

One Friday evening, when I was about eight, having grown bored with whatever was on TV, I played in my bedroom with my younger brother. We heard a strange gurgling noise coming from the nearby bathroom, and, hearing it a second time, we rushed to the den to tell my parents.

"Jiggle the handle on the commode," my mother instructed from the couch.

"It's not running," I said. "It sounds like it's bubbling up."

Deciding to investigate, my father walked to the bathroom and switched on the light in time to see brown waste rising in the toilet bowl. As it neared the crest, he grabbed the plush pink bathmat and shoved it down into the opening, hoping to stop the flow, but soon sewage overflowed onto the pink tile floor.

"Go get Mama," Dad yelled, nearly elbow-deep in the toilet bowl.

Mom came and quickly spread dirty towels from the hamper to keep the mess confined to one room. Excited by the drama rising from a previously dull Friday night, I ran to check the second bathroom.

"It's coming out of the commode and up through the bathtub drain!" I reported.

And it kept coming. Despite my parents' efforts, the wood floors and area rugs in most of the house were soon coated with a layer of sludgy brown liquid. My brother's favorite toy, a large black-and-white stuffed horse, was soaked in the mess.

The odor of diluted human waste was surprisingly mild, like being downwind of a sewer rather than in one.

"Don't stand in that!" my father shouted. Bewildered, I looked unsuccessfully for a place to stand that was not "in that." My parents were horrified. They tried shutting the water off, but that didn't help, nor did their attempts to plug all the drains. I, understanding little about bacteria or the labor and expense of cleanup, was mostly just intrigued.

After futile efforts with mops and buckets, and after several phone calls, my parents learned that a malfunction with the city's sewer system, combined with paved-over manhole covers on our street, had caused the backup in the house. Then they placed a call to my aunts up the road, who were just getting home from their shift at the mill.

Aunt Louise drove down to collect us children around 11 p.m. We were to spend the night at her house so my parents could sort things out at home.

We probably stank, and we were certainly disoriented and tired. Rather than insisting that we take baths, my two aunts invited us to sit on their mostly white sofas, drink Cokes with them, and watch a black-and-white war movie on TV. Their white miniature French poodles, Gigi and Don Juan, knowing small people to be unpredictable, eyed us suspiciously from the kitchen with their rheumy eyes. These dogs outwardly resembled my two aunts—Aunt Louise's dog, Don Juan, was taller and thin; Aunt Ella's Gigi was shorter and round—but they lacked my aunts' pleasant dispositions.

I'd never stayed up to watch the late-night movie before. I don't remember the title, but the movie's plot involved a young, orphaned Asian boy, maybe my age, who was offered protection by some American troops during World War II. As it turned out, though, the brave young boy was as much help to the troops as they were to him.

"There's nothing sissy about him, is there!" Aunt Louise said to us, admiringly.

Undisturbed by our late-night presence in her childless home, Aunt Louise smoked her cigarettes and unwound from her shift until the movie ended. Then she packed us off to share one bed while she and Aunt Ella shared the other.

In retrospect, I realize that sugary, caffeinated beverages and a war movie are not the best things to offer a displaced child at midnight, and a bath would certainly have been sensible. But at the time, I found no fault with my aunts' hospitality.

City workers came to help with the cleanup the next day, under my mother's nagging supervision. The city also paid for the orange and brown shag carpeting that soon covered the damaged wood floors throughout most of our house. But for a long time after, I thought I still detected that faint stench of sewage rising.

✦ ✦ ✦

Much later, I learned that, as a younger woman, Aunt Louise had handled figurative shit equally in stride. My mother often shared stories about her family, and I admired the closeness of the women, always in each other's business and always having each other's backs. Mom's mother, aunts, and grandmother lived near one another, often next door, in a series of rented houses; to the annoyance of their husbands, they came and went without knocking and frequently advised one another about childrearing. This closeness extended into my mother's generation. My grandmother and her two unmarried daughters shared a house, and Mom talked to them daily by phone.

Mom was a child when Great Aunt Louise was a young woman, but she nevertheless remembered the details about Louise's ill-fated marriage, her memory heightened by sisterly gossip and repetition in the years afterward.

In the early 1940s, at age twenty-five, Louise married Dave Booker and soon regretted it. Unfortunately, throughout the first half of the twentieth century, South Carolina had the distinction of being the only state in which divorce was illegal. According to the South Carolina legislators of this time, even if the bed you made was physically dangerous or deserted by your spouse, you must continue to lie in it.

Before marriage, Louise lived with her mother, stepfather, Ella, and Ella's son Dale. My grandparents had bought a place of their own by then, and their family had grown to include five children. Louise dated other young men before Dave, but none of them were serious. Often they took Sunday drives, sometimes double-dating with Ella, who was eight years older than Louise, sometimes with a group of cousins and friends, and sometimes with just Ella and Dale tagging along. Their trips were often to state parks, and sometimes included amateur photo sessions, so my mother inherited an album filled with black-and-white images of Louise, Ella, and other young adults posed on rocky outcroppings or sitting on blankets beside a lake. By this time, Ella had saved up enough to buy a used car with a rumble seat, and many of the shots featured Ella or Louise standing on the running board or perched pin-up style on the fender of this vehicle.

After Dave came into the picture, the picnics and Sunday drives continued, sometimes accompanied by Ella, usually in Dave's car. But, this time, Louise adored Dave, a tall, burly, handsome man who loved liquor and horses. She savored the feel of his biceps under her hands, the smell of cigarettes on his clothes, the timbre of his voice as she rested her ear against his chest. Her father had died when she was a baby, and her stepfather, who entered Louise's life when she was about ten, had always seemed caring but distant. In the beginning, with Dave, she felt at home.

When they married, he vowed to support her, and she would stay home to take care of the house. They lived in a small duplex with Louise's mother and stepfather on the other side.

Dave managed riding stables on the outskirts of Columbia and sometimes drove a taxi for additional income. Each night when the stables closed for the day, Louise counted up his earnings and prepared it for deposit. Before long, however, she realized that Dave converted much of their money to whisky. He often spent evenings out with other men and returned home stumbling drunk. But his drinking wasn't the only problem. Although Louise considered her husband irresistible, she soon recognized that he looked at her body with distaste.

Sitting around kitchen tables or on worn sofas, over coffee and cigarettes, she shared her frustrations with her female kin.

"When we're in bed together," Louise complained, "it's like he's chasing something out of reach. He's straining for some feeling, but I don't know what it is. Instead of making us feel closer, I end up feeling alone."

"That's just your imagination," her mother advised. "It's always better for the man."

But Dave soon voiced his disappointment bitterly. Once, months after their marriage, they lay sweaty on top of rumpled sheets in their dark bedroom after making love. The hot, humid night air and the sound of cicadas drifted through the open window, and an electric fan whirred on the dresser. For a time, each was quiet and introspective.

Then, "Cover yo' nasty self up!" ordered Dave, before rolling over to sleep. The disgust in his voice stunned Louise out of her own thoughts, his words stinging like a slap and bringing tears to her eyes. She didn't know how to respond, so she didn't. She slid under the sheet and seethed with silent anger and humiliation.

She broke her silence in the company of sisters and mother, who shared her outrage.

"There's something unnatural about that man," Louise's mother commiserated.

But Louise blamed herself at first, assessing her waist and breasts, reviewing her hygiene routine, hoping to find the fixable flaw. She knew she wasn't perfect, but in the mirror she saw a trim waist, long legs, and a girl who kept herself neat and clean, even if she couldn't afford to be fancy. The cigarettes helped her keep off the weight, and her naturally curly hair framed her high, bronzed cheekbones to advantage.

Ruby lipstick plumped her thin lips, and she resolved to wear it more often.

Her strongest ally was her eldest niece, Mae. Away from the other women, teasing but confident, she said, "Louise, you're the ripest tomato on the block, and if Dave doesn't like the flavor, we'll find someone who does."

At the time of Louise's marriage, Mae was just seventeen and had recently quit school. Never a beauty, she had grown into a tall and stocky young woman with a sharp chin and a slight overbite. She wore low heels and shirtwaist dresses meant to minimize her height and girth. Her long experience helping her mother run the house and care for her younger siblings, including my mother, had made her more mature than her years. Louise thought of this opinionated, independent girl as more of a sister than a niece.

As Dave stayed away from home more and more, often overnight, Mae began to advise her aunt.

"You can't depend on him. You better set you some money aside." At Mae's suggestion, Louise began taking a few crumpled bills from the riding stable's proceeds each night and tucking them away in her pocketbook.

I imagine that Dave had been running the stables haphazardly, showing up in the late morning and staying for a few hours at a time. Finally, when Louise stopped by one afternoon to collect the day's income, the usually-absent owner told her Dave had been fired.

Her husband didn't return home all week, and the rent was due, so Louise used what she had set aside to pay the balance. He'd stayed away for a night or two before, so she was more angry than worried.

After paying the rent, she sat at the kitchen table with her mother, sister, and Mae. They drank Coca Colas, Louise and Mae smoked, and they worked Dave into hamburger in their verbal meat grinder. Self-righteous feminine anger floated in the smoke-thickened air between the table and the ceiling light.

"I'll be damned before I go huntin' for that man in some honkytonk!" Louise fumed. "I bet he's off with another woman."

"Well, I don't think so," said her mother. "I talked to Eddie out on the sidewalk today." Eddie was the tall, handsome sixteen-year-old boy who sometimes did yard work for the neighbors.

"He said, 'Miz Campbell, Dave Booker is a sonofabitch, and I'm sorry Louise is married to him.' I asked if he'd seen him, and he said, 'I've seen more of him than I ever cared to, and I hope I never see him again.' And then he just hurried off, like he knew more than he was sayin'."

Each woman had a theory about what Dave had said or done to Eddie. But Louise wasted no more time with tears or indecision.

"We both need jobs of our own," she told Mae as they sat at the table. Mae had worked part-time at the dime store and helped at home since leaving school. Her father suffered from heart problems, and Louise knew that Mae could help her parents more by earning money than by doing household chores.

The next day, Mae and Louise went to the mill where Ella already worked, and they were immediately hired on the second shift. In wartime, jobs were plentiful and wages climbed. I picture them riding the city bus together five afternoons each week, carrying bag lunches in the pocketbooks slung at their elbows and wearing cotton scarfs over their hair to keep it clean. They entered at the front of the three-story red-brick building, laughing and chatting with other workers as they passed the watchman, and punched the time clock as their shifts began. The building's tall ceilings and many windows were intended to minimize the heat, but in summer, the workers emptied into the night wet with sweat.

Dave was not yet gone for good, however. The details of his homecoming did not make their way into the stories my mother heard and passed on to me, but I imagine him returning wounded in spirit, sick from alcohol, meeting Louise's tearful accusations with his own tearful, at the time sincere, apologies and promises of reform. She took him back.

He went back to driving his taxi, and Louise continued her work at the mill. Then, one evening while Louise worked, her mother paused as she entered her side of the duplex. She heard Dave's voice beyond the covered living room window on the other side. He had not been home when she had left, and she suspected he'd been drinking rather than working.

"That feels good, doesn't it?" Dave chuckled throatily.

"You know it does," responded another male voice. A chair in the living room banged a few times against the floor, wood on wood.

She stood paralyzed, listening a minute or two before walking into her side of the duplex and slamming the door.

"I think that's a horrible thing for a man to do to a woman," my mother said, years later, as she told me about this episode, indignation infusing her voice even then. "He knew he was attracted to other men, but he married Louise anyway and ruined her life."

And I can certainly see her point. In the traditional union that Louise, my mother, and—they believed—God expected, marriage consisted of financial support from the man, domestic care and comfort from the woman, sexual intimacy between them, and, eventually, children. Louise was bound until death to a partner with whom these goals were unobtainable.

But I also think about what it must have been like to be gay in the 1940s South. Like light-skinned African Americans who chose to pass as white in order to avoid the discrimination of their racist society, many gays passed as heterosexual to avoid bigotry and persecution. In that era of involuntary committal to psychiatric institutions to "cure" homosexuality, aversion therapy was often delivered via electrodes connected to the genitals. Even if the person was not locked up, he risked losing his job and bringing shame to himself and his family. As late as 1976, the attorney general of South Carolina stated that homosexuality was a legitimate reason to refuse someone employment or to fire an employee. Even in 2018, South Carolina state representatives filed a bill to make marriage available only to heterosexual couples after the U.S. Supreme Court declared such laws unconstitutional.

And I think about my own child: smart, creative, beautiful, and pansexual. A term that didn't even exist in the 1940s, pansexual means that one's sexual attraction is not limited to people of a certain biological sex or gender, including transgender. Blair identifies as non-binary (neither wholly male nor female) and prefers the plural, gender-neutral pronoun. As a high school senior, they posted exuberantly on social media about the friend who asked them to the homecoming dance; later, they posted a picture of them both wearing matching bow ties, white shirts, and black sport coats. I admire my child's openness and bravery, defiantly themself in all situations.

More recently, just days before going off to the arty, private college where their gender identity and sexuality will be welcomed, Blair walked into my bedroom as I got ready to sleep and sat on the edge of my bed. Their short, orange-dyed hair glowed like a fiery halo above their black Frank Iero T-shirt and dark-gray skinny jeans.

"So, what's new in your life?" Blair began awkwardly.

I had come to recognize this conversation starter as a prelude to Blair telling me about something new in their life. Never much of a talker, my oldest child still occasionally consented to cuddling on the couch. We had spent the last few hours sitting almost silently together and watching TV.

"Not much, how about you?"

"I've been thinking that I might want to start gender therapy," they said.

I felt a tightening of worry in my diaphragm, which I attempted to quell with measured breathing. Trying to emphasize my parental curiosity and downplay my parental anxiety, I said, "Tell me what gender therapy is and how someone gets it."

I learned that it involves working with a psychological counselor who specializes in this area. The counselor, like all good ones, helps the client better understand their own sense of self and make healthy decisions based on that understanding. One such decision may be to transition to a different outward gender than the one they were born with, in which case the counselor helps the client find appropriate resources to navigate that transition. Blair, I noticed, had put a lot of thought not only into this decision, but also into how to broach it to me in terms I could relate to.

"I went online and found some gender therapists in Boston that accept our insurance." By this time, I was more shocked by Blair's uncharacteristic practicality than by the notion of gender therapy. This was the kid whom I had hounded daily less than a year ago just to get them to register for standardized tests, fill out college applications, check for email responses, and solicit reference letters. I was proud of this sign of their growing maturity, comforted by this evidence of my young adult's impending self-sufficiency.

"I think the counseling is a good idea," I said. "I'll pay for whatever insurance doesn't cover."

Attitudes toward sexuality have changed for the better since Dave and Louise were married, yet my child will still need the strength to handle a larger than average share of life's messes. Despite their growing capabilities, every day I worry about them being judged, condemned, even hurt.

Because Dave feared these things too, he hid his identity and drank away his pain, and, if he ruined anyone's life, it was his own. As I said, Louise could handle shit, and she refused to succumb to ruin.

By this time, she hoped Dave would not come home, and she soon got her wish. The next time rent was due, Mae told her, "You're crazy to pay rent in somebody else's name."

The landlord's office was a small trailer plopped in the middle of a gravel-covered vacant lot downtown. Mae and Louise stopped there on their way to work one afternoon. The heavy, middle-aged, balding man sat behind a small metal desk examining a newspaper. He looked up and smiled as the two women came in, but his smile fell when he heard that Louise wanted the lease in her name.

"Oh, come on now!" he said, in a tone at once reassuring and dismissive. "Y'all will work things out before long. You don't want to go to all that trouble changing things. When y'all make up, I'll just have to change it right back."

He met Louise's protests with a wave of the hand, and Mae had had enough. "Come on, Louise. There's plenty of other places to rent." She grasped her aunt by the elbow and drew her toward the door. As they turned to go, the landlord spoke.

"Wait a minute." He swiveled his wooden chair toward the file cabinet behind him, found the lease under B, and turned back to the desk as he tore the paper in half.

"Mr. Booker no longer rents from me," he said, smiling again. "Mrs. Booker, we'll fill out the new paperwork right now."

Louise, Mae, and Ella continued to work at the mill, finding satisfaction in the money they earned and in the company of family. Louise, still in her twenties, knew that divorce was not an option for her. Some South Carolinians went to other states for divorces, but they had to establish residency first. It took twelve months to do this in nearby Georgia, and even if she had the money, Louise would not have wanted to leave her family. When a bill allowing divorce in South Carolina came before the legislature in 1945, it was defeated, so Louise resigned herself to a lifetime of estrangement.

But one night, when she returned home from work, her mother met her at the door. "Louise, you've got company," she said, standing in the screen door on her side of the duplex.

Louise opened her door and walked cautiously inside. Lying on her bed beneath the covers, she found Dave in his undershirt and trousers, unshaven, with bloodshot eyes, looking older and frailer than she remembered. The whole bedroom smelled of stale alcohol and sweat.

"Louise, I'm sick and I've come home to die," he declared mournfully.

She hadn't seen him in a year, and disappointment had hardened her. "You'll have to die somewhere else," she replied. She narrowed one eye as she spoke and punctuated her words with a slight toss of her head. "If you don't get outta that bed, I'm going to call the law."

The look in her eye, the tone of her voice, the set of her jaw: something told him she meant it. He collected his hat, shirt, and shoes and crossed the porch a final time under the glowering eyes of Louise's kin.

Fortunately for Louise, lawyers and legislators continued to lobby, and the constitutional change that would allow divorce in South Carolina for reasons of adultery, cruelty, excessive drunkenness, or desertion was finally approved in 1949.

Louise knew immediately that she wanted her legal freedom. Saving the money, filing the paperwork, and enduring the necessary waiting period took her about two years, and Louise was divorced by 1952. She never married again; her sister Ella and her niece Mae also remained single. Independent and hardworking the rest of their lives, they enjoyed the constancy and companionship of family women.

Of the many types of love, I hope these women ended up with the one they wanted—that, rather than silently longing for a partner, they felt happiest in their sisterly bond. I also hope Dave found a way to share lasting intimacy with a lover he desired. And in my vision of the world as it should be, a vein of shit-handling fortitude flows from Aunt Louise and Mae, through me, and straight to my child. This strength will allow them to withstand adversity and discover their true love, whoever that will be.

— 5 —

Rosalee's Commitment

My aunt haunts me—her ghost drawn to me because now, after fifty years of neglect, I alone devote pages of paper to her, though not origamied into houses and clothes.

—Maxine Hong Kingston, *The Woman Warrior*

Behind one of the facilities owned by the South Carolina Department of Mental Health in Columbia lies a graveyard surrounded by a chain-link fence. Unlike most cemeteries, with their arrays of geometric stones projecting from the ground as testaments of loss and love, this one holds only rows of flat rectangular granite, each stone about the size of a small mailbox. Here lie hundreds of the hospital's dead, arranged chronologically and dating back more than a century, the earliest ones engraved with only a number. After finding the graveyard's location online, I drove there believing that I would not be able to go beyond the fence. "Not open to the public," one site had said. But I found the gate unlocked, and seeing no one nearby, I went inside, thinking that I could always ask forgiveness in lieu of permission.

Runners of centipede grass encroached on the markers nearest the gate; these stones were stained by dirt and dotted with moss and lichen, so I knew they marked the cemetery's oldest inhabitants. I walked across the grass, scanning the rows until I found, at some point in the twentieth century, the stones had been engraved with the deceased patients' names and dates of death. I found the one I had been looking for, Rosalee Pittman, 1998, near the far-left corner of the yard.

I met Rosalee only a few times. I remember visiting her once at the State Hospital on Bull Street with my mother and grandmother when I was about ten years old. Rosalee lived there with her middle-aged son, James, which I thought was nice for the two of them.

Most of the adult conversation of that day persists in my memory only as gray background noise, but the visual and tactile sensations remain vivid. On that May afternoon, the temperature neared ninety, and gnats assaulted my eyes and nose. In the humid air, my hair grew frizzier and stickier to the touch, and I sweated in my jeans. "Think about something else," my mother said. But I couldn't. I flapped my hands in front of my face, exciting the gnats, and I repeatedly fingered my hair, making it messier. I was curious about this new place, but I also longed to be home watching *I Dream of Jeannie* reruns. My mother and grandmother brought my brother and me along to this family open house because they thought we were too young to stay home alone.

Rosalee and James both had faded ginger hair and wore glasses, and Rosalee's jaws sank in because she had lost all of her teeth. Her voice sounded muffled, and she moved as if her Nursemates shoes were weighted with iron soles. She was my grandmother's sister, about ten years younger. Her family had her committed a few years after her husband died, in the 1950s, when she was in her mid-thirties. On the day of my visit, she must have been about sixty. As a child, I didn't know why she had been sent to the asylum. She just seemed old, quiet, and, I assumed, crazy. Now I wonder how much a woman had to drink, how many men she had to bed, how violently and frequently she had to swear, before a mental institution seemed the answer.

Whatever her disorder, I don't believe it was caused by grief at her husband's death, despite the fact that the commitment followed on the heels of his demise. He was fifteen years her senior, and she had married him when she was about eighteen, probably because she was pregnant. I have a creased, black-and-white photo from the 1930s or '40s of Rosalee standing next to this man in a grassy field. Rosalee wears her hair in a simple bob, the height of fashion from more than a decade before. Her cotton drop-waist dress and white stockings contribute to her youthful appearance. Her husband looks even more out of date, with his hair parted down the middle, a thick mustache, and a white shirt and dark trousers that appear too big for him. They both stare at the camera, suppressing smiles, and Rosalee's hand is draped casually on his shoulder. Instead of wife and husband, they look like a gangly, teenaged girl posing next to her grownup brother who is visiting for a holiday.

On Sundays, before they married, this thirty-three-year-old man walked Rosalee to Sandy Level Baptist Church, where both families worshiped irregularly; sometimes they took a circuitous route, and sometimes they didn't make it there at all, foregoing the sermon for the stealthy pleasure of a blanket laid on pine needles beyond the low cemetery wall. They would quickly have two children, James—who eventually lived with Rosalee at the State Hospital—and a daughter, Joyce, born about two years later.

Before the husband's illness, he and Rosalee spent their leisure hours drinking cheap whiskey in their tiny house on his father's land and fighting loudly enough for their relatives next door to hear. On the surface, they fought over casual daily slights—she told him he needed to wash; he said she used to be pretty. But deeper down, they resented their own weaknesses, which they projected onto spouse and children as if they were pinning fabric onto dress dummies.

Evenings, he swayed on the twilit front porch—amid the cast-off chair with ripped upholstery, spare parts from a junked car, and the crank wringer from a broken washing machine—profanely menacing his son, daughter, and their parasite-infested dog. I imagine they all learned to hide until they could decide from the tone of his rants if they'd be safer out of sight or braving his fury now so he wouldn't come out and find them.

In 1952, after a lengthy illness, he died of malignant hypertension and uremia, the result of long-term intemperance and lack of medical care, according to the death certificate. Rosalee, only about thirty then, still pretty in a coarse way, was at once too young and too dissipated to be a decent widow.

She and her children moved from the country to a small rented house in Columbia, where she found work as a laundromat attendant. Her children had long since learned to entertain themselves, and at home, she craved companionship as much as she craved alcohol. Every drop Rosalee swallowed tasted like more, and she did not want to drink alone. She would have liked to be respectable, but she lacked moderation and impulse control. Most of all, though, Rosalee lacked the ability to sit with herself, to face all the fragments of feeling that teemed within her, and to shape them into a coherent self she could accept the burden of.

Of course, people would talk about a woman like this. Men she knew would tell their friends, who would then come calling, smiling, offering liquor and company. They'd come to the door, hats in hand, at Saturday's dusk. Sometimes she accompanied a man to a ramshackle bar, but more often than not, they drank in porch chairs or at the kitchen table, laughing more and louder into the evening.

At the end of the night, sometimes the man followed her to bed, if he timed his advances right: after the onset of artificial intimacy but before the crying jag began. Neighbors whispered, and the shame Rosalee should have felt besieged her family, especially her brothers, who couldn't keep their sister in line. Because they believed that most women were vulnerable to sexual transgression if not properly controlled, a loose woman always implied a weak man. If she had no husband, the responsibility and the blame fell on the closest male relative. And then there were the children to think about.

Bob, the oldest brother and a cop, tried to bully her into acting right if she didn't have enough pride to do it herself.

"You're a sot and a slut!

"You got no business carrying on like this!

"You won't be satisfied 'til you're in jail or dead, and you're dragging those children right along with you!

"You're a mother, and you need to act like it!"

Through many of these harangues, Rosalee sat on the worn-out sofa, resting her head in her hand; her reddish hair, slightly dirty and disheveled, framed her head like a burning halo.

"What do mothers act like, Bob?" she asked tiredly.

"Like your mother did. They stay home and they take care of their children, take care of the house." Rosalee was the fifth of her parents' six children, born when her mother was almost forty. Her father died when Rosalee was fifteen, leaving the mother to finish raising the youngest ones alone.

"My children are big enough to take care of themselves, and this house ain't mine, anyway."

But sometimes, I've been told, Rosalee cried bitter tears of shame, hating herself for her behavior. Other times she swore at Bob and hurled an ashtray or picture frame. On these occasions, he slammed her door behind him, hurling back over his shoulder the prediction that he'd lock her up himself one day.

James, a teenager by this time, was almost never home. He seldom went to school, sometimes worked odd jobs, and slept at friends' or relatives' houses or out of doors. When Rosalee's belly rounded with another baby, father unknown, Brother Bob arranged for twelve-year-old Joyce to enter foster care. I don't know what sort of family she ended up with or why he didn't take the girl into his own home. He may have feared that Joyce, given her upbringing, would negatively influence his own son, just a year or two older; he may have wanted to avoid the complications of having two opposite-sex teenagers in his house, even though they were cousins; or he may simply have thought adding another child was too much expense and trouble.

Alone, sometimes Rosalee cried when the liquor wore off and her life seemed an empty cycle of work at the laundromat, four dingy walls, and loneliness. She cradled her cracked picture frames and missed her children. She loved them, but her mental illness, her attempts at self-medication through drinking, and her resulting alcoholism made her unable to show it consistently.

I believe that Rosalee must have suffered from something like bipolar disorder. Although I don't know exactly what that's like, I've struggled with depression all my life and used to try to drink away anxiety and despair. Sadly, although it took away my pain for brief periods of time, it left me submerged in shame, regret, and even deeper melancholy. These feelings amplified when I considered the lasting pain I may have inflicted on my vulnerable children, who may one day be forced to exorcise demons I planted in them. Nothing like the antidepressants that I rely on now was available to Rosalee, and I often think, *There but for the grace of God—and modern medicine—go I.*

In late 1953, a year or two before the asylum, Rosalee and the baby moved in with my grandmother and grandfather and their two grown children, one of whom was my father, about age twenty. The three-bedroom house was too small for all of them, and Rosalee could not give up her nightlife. Grandmother was a moral woman and, like her brother, she worried about the approval of others. And she still had an unmarried daughter to consider. Her lectures were quieter than Bob's, buttressed by unanswerable questions rather than accusations.

"Aren't you ashamed?

"When are you going to settle down and start acting right?

"Do you think God is pleased with the way you've been carrying on?"

In response, Rosalee sometimes bowed her head and asked forgiveness, and at other times, she cursed, tipped over the dark wooden coffee table, and slammed the door as she left.

Then, without saying goodbye, Rosalee ran off one day with a man she barely knew, leaving the baby behind. No one knew where she'd gone; Bob, even with his police connections, couldn't track her down.

After months had passed and it seemed that Rosalee would not be coming back, my grandmother and grandfather knew they couldn't keep the child. They were poor and getting old. Bob made calls, and soon the boy was adopted by a good family in Orangeburg. I never met him, but my father must have kept up with Rosalee's youngest. He called him many years later to tell him of his mother's death.

About a year after she'd disappeared, Rosalee returned to Columbia alone. She was furious when she discovered the child was gone. I don't know if she ever saw him again, but I know they wouldn't let her see him then. Alcoholism had made her temper more volatile, and she unleashed it on my grandmother, breaking her furniture and china figurines, vomiting obscenities and accusations.

No one knew how to control her. So, at the family's request, a judge ruled that Rosalee was unfit to care for herself and committed her to the state asylum.

James joined her at the State Hospital some years later when it became evident that he was slow to learn and hard to manage. He was simple, and, although he meant no harm, he had a bad temper like Rosalee. After some minor legal trouble and difficulty keeping a job, Bob thought the state hospital would be the easiest way to keep him safe and fed. My grandmother visited them regularly, and sometimes one or both of them stayed at her house for a weekend.

After Rosalee's commitment, Joyce stayed in contact with her mother's relatives and fared better than her older brother. When I was a small girl, probably years before my State Hospital visit, twenty-something-year-old Joyce lived for several months at my grandparents' house, sleeping on the single bed in the spare room, like a nun in a convent cell, while she studied cosmetology at Midlands Technical Community College. My family often visited for Sunday dinner, and I saw her there. I didn't know about her mother's history at the time, and I liked her look: tall and pretty, capable and sweet, with chestnut hair curled around her head, makeup on her lips and eyes. She didn't talk much to me because I was a small, quiet child, but I was fascinated with this seemingly isolated, beautiful young woman. Certainly not a child like me, but not old like my parents, she was a closer version of what I hoped to be.

Then, one Sunday when we visited, Joyce was gone. My grandfather said she had left early that morning on the train for home. My child's brain had assumed that this was home for

Joyce now, but it adjusted quickly to the news that it was not. Did she go all by herself, I wondered?

"And do you know, when she left, she was carrying a suitcase and wearing leather boots that were this high," my grandfather said, holding his hand beside my knee cap.

I marveled at the idea, connecting his words with the train ride, with leaving alone, with this not being home. Joyce was from another town in South Carolina, but I didn't know exactly where or with whom she lived.

I don't recall ever seeing Joyce and her mother together, and I don't know if Rosalee was proud of her daughter. But that day, I had the sense that Joyce had accomplished some feat, and that her journey was taking her into a new life. I pictured her standing on a train platform, preparing to board in her tall boots, beautiful, sturdy, purposeful, and free. Joyce's image has stayed with me all these years because a part of me also chases that train to freedom, while a shadowy side is drawn to follow her mother's footsteps instead.

✦ ✦ ✦

On the day we visited Rosalee at the hospital, we all sat outside on folding chairs in the acres-wide sandy yard between the main hospital building, which had been a cutting-edge facility in the 1820s, and the twelve-foot brick perimeter wall. Several other smaller buildings stood to the far left and the far right of the main building. A few old pin oaks and some sparse centipede grass grew on the grounds, and we had to place our chairs carefully to avoid anthills.

My mother, who wanted everyone to feel comfortable, to pretend it wasn't awkward, said, "Looks like they're going to have some music over there," as three men set up stands and brass instruments about fifty yards away. "It turned out to be a hot day, but at least we didn't get rain." Her small talk was a nervous habit, but this visit was emotionally low-stakes for her. Rosalee was only her relation by marriage.

Grandmother filled Rosalee and James in on the recent events of other family members' lives—someone's operation, someone starting school, someone having a baby—and the older women talked about memories from childhood.

Rosalee wore a thin, faded blue housedress that buttoned up the front and flat white shoes. Her breasts and stomach sagged, and she looked a lot like my grandmother, except perhaps older (she wasn't) and frailer. I don't recall her speaking much, not at all to me, although I imagine she must have said hello. The only way to reconcile my memory of the woman I saw then with my impression of the woman Rosalee had been long ago is to factor in the flattening effects of heavy mood-altering medications and hard time. In her youth and early adulthood, Rosalee must have been vibrant, attractive, and intense. This Rosalee was vacant, muted, and spent.

While the adults talked, I watched people as if they moved inside a television screen. The hospital grounds were fascinatingly unfamiliar, but I felt somewhat removed in time and place. Some of the residents had obvious physical or mental disabilities: they sat in wheelchairs with mouths drooping or paced the yard frenetically. Others, like Rosalee and James, just looked sad, or slovenly, or old. I wondered how the staff would know who belonged inside and who belonged outside when it came time to go. Somehow they did. We left that afternoon, but Rosalee and James remained behind the hospital's brick wall.

+ + +

Although I saw her only a few times, Rosalee has always intrigued me. She was our family's Bertha Mason, the madwoman confined to the attic in Charlotte Brontë's *Jane Eyre*. She defied authority and was punished for it, something I did repeatedly as a teenager, almost as unsubtly as Rosalee. Unlike her, I managed to test the borders between sexual precocity and promiscuity and between experimentation and addiction without crossing them.

I should say that Rosalee has interested me when I wasn't completely absorbed with myself. One particularly self-absorbed period occurred during my early twenties, when I was going through my first divorce. I had married my high-school boyfriend at nineteen, against everyone's advice—everyone except my father, who urged me to hurry down the aisle before I wound up pregnant. Smart, kind, handsomely blonde, and nerdy, this boy graduated from high school when I was a sophomore. We went on to the same college, and he eventually began a Ph.D. program in math while I worked on my undergrad degree.

Then, the summer before my senior year of college, I experienced a crisis, which crystallized strangely around a character on *The Tracey Ullman Show*, a popular comedy variety show at that time. One of Ullman's many characters was a frumpy, middle-aged office worker named Kay, who lived with her elderly mother. Despite her affability, Kay's naivete, outdated wardrobe, and awkward social skills made her the frequent butt of jokes. To play this character, Ullman wore long-sleeved blouses with Peter Pan collars buttoned to the neck and several inches of padding under polyester slacks. In an era of big hair, Kay had a conservative, androgynous bob. In one episode, she vacations at a singles resort, and while others indulge in casual sex, she wins a hat weaving competition and swaps her prize hat for a chaste kiss from a new friend.

Despite my teenage indiscretions, I worried that others saw me as a Kay, and, worse, I feared this was who I was. Shy and married, at twenty-one, I felt middle-aged, out of touch, lonely, and pathetic. Irrationally, I blamed my husband and my family for my self-loathing, and I began an insensitive campaign to escape my situation.

Fearing I was fat, like Kay, and also worried about money, I exercised obsessively and starved myself with regimented allowances of food, mostly salad and yogurt, until I stalled at a size four. I convinced my husband he should eat less, too, to save money, and we both became gaunt and miserable. Combatting Kay's asexuality, I nursed a crush on one of my husband's friends, and when the friend rejected me, I wept, drunk and hysterical, on the bathroom floor of our apartment, my head in my husband's lap as he sat on the edge of the bathtub comforting me. I felt trapped by my marriage.

Without understanding it, I still craved another man to accept the burden of me, to be the scaffold that steadied my shaky sense of self.

Shortly after this marriage ended, I graduated from college. Instead of boarding a train like Joyce, I scrounged and borrowed money and boarded a flight to Europe. I got a student work visa and spent the six months after graduation working as a temp secretary in London and traveling with other young people. In short, I ran away.

In Europe, I saw rats, castles, cathedrals, London Bridge, and the Eiffel Tower, earned pounds instead of dollars, rode the Tube late at night, walked across parts of southern Spain, developed a slight British accent, drank pints of lager in local pubs, fell in love with an Australian boy, and dated a forty-year-old, married father of two. I lived in a London row house with eleven other twenty-somethings from America, Canada, Australia, and New Zealand, and then, briefly, in a tenement squat with a smaller subset of those same people. This would have been the ideal time to strengthen my shaky sense of self, but instead I searched for another scaffold. Then, at twenty-five, I embarked on marriage number two to a handsome young man with rich parents and a well-developed substance abuse problem, an irresistible combination.

As I worked to tear my first marriage apart, simultaneously tearing my young husband apart to convince myself it was his fault, Rosalee found love. I learned about this chapter of her life only recently, having been too preoccupied to pay attention when it occurred. When she was nearly seventy, she fell in love with a fellow patient, a man about whom I know almost nothing. The hospital staff sympathized with their romance, and when the couple wished to marry, they argued on Rosalee's behalf to obtain my grandmother's permission as next of kin, Bob having passed on years earlier. Whatever the reason for his hospitalization, Rosalee's husband soon got better and was discharged, with Rosalee released to his care.

I imagine her then, experiencing the world like a normal woman for the first time in nearly forty years, with a partner and a home of her own. I hope their late-life love was sweet and comforting. I hope they experienced joy that redeemed years of suffering. All that I know for sure, though, is that their love was brief. Rosalee's new husband died within a few years of their marriage, and, unable to care for herself, Rosalee returned to the custody of South Carolina's Department of Mental Health, where her son still resided.

Rosalee outlived both her husband and my grandmother by a few years. When she died, my father tried to arrange for her burial next to her first husband at Sandy Level Baptist Church Cemetery, where they used to walk so many years ago, where my grandmother and many other family members are also buried. But a cousin who owned the plot refused to allow it, so she was buried by the state with other unclaimed bodies in the graveyard behind the hospital.

Today, this cemetery is running out of room, but Rosalee lies placidly in her assigned row, not too far from the eight-foot chain-link fence.

— 6 —

Not about My Mother

This chapter is not about my mother because my mother is not a misfit Southern woman. In many ways, when it comes to the expectations for southern women, my mother, Joanne, embodies the rule that proves the exceptions.

She had four children and, throughout our growing up, wife and mother were her only occupations. Actually, she did work part-time for less than a year when my younger brother and I were in high school and my older siblings were out of the house. She was hired at the customer service desk of J. B. White's department store, where she enjoyed the comaraderie and the employee discount, and spent most of her modest earnings in the store. But she quit that job shortly after I brought my boyfriend home after school one afternoon when no one was home. Our neighbor phoned my father at work to report the presence of a car she didn't recognize, and my father called our house to tell me to send him home.

I didn't hear him ask her to quit, but she told me later that he did. When we were alone, I asked if this was because of me; had my selfish misbehavior cost her the job she enjoyed?

"No," she said, smiling. "It wasn't about you. He said I wasn't keeping the house up, that I was neglecting my job at home. And he's right. It was just too much."

Care-taking, self-sacrifice, and domesticity define the ideal southern woman. But my mother also possessed the southern woman's secret weapon of expressing herself through indirection. After I had moved out of state, had two children, and visited South Carolina roughly twice a year, she made a point during each visit of pointing out the weight I'd gained without actually saying it.

For example, once after I'd bought some new clothes, she asked me the size. When I told her I wore a 10, she looked at me skeptically. "Do you wear a 10 in *everything*?" she asked, as if I'd located a monstrously oversized 10, but in everything else I would need a 12 or 14.

On another visit, she said, "Now those pants look good on you. You should get some more like that," the emphasis suggesting that every other pair I wore made me look like a water buffalo.

When I cut my hair in a chin-length bob, she said, "Do you think it's too short? You might need a little more hair for your face." That one was pretty direct.

Chastity and modesty are other key features of an ideal Southern woman. My mother married at age 20 and was a virgin on her wedding night. She told me a story once about having been so nervous on her week-long honeymoon that she became constipated and had to buy a bottle of laxative. When she got home, her unmarried sisters came over to visit and help her unpack. They saw the laxative and teased her about the sexual anxiety it exposed. I picture the two sisters, Mae and Carrie, older than my mother but still in their twenties, sitting on her bed with the open suitcase between them. Joanne moved from suitcase to closet to drawers, laughing with them as they plucked up the blue bottle, held it high, and affectionately teased her about a rite of passage that they themselves had never experienced.

So, because of how well she fit, this chapter is not about my mother. It is about my mother's sister Carrie, my maiden aunt, who did not fulfill the role of the ideal southern woman because she never married and had children, but who otherwise stayed within the bounds of expectations. You could say that this piece is also about the narrowness of those bounds.

By the time I finished college, Aunt Carrie was in her late 50s and Aunt Mae was in her early sixties; they lived with my grandmother, as they had their whole lives. My grandfather died sometime before I was born. My aunts had both taken disability retirement, Carrie from her work as a dental assistant and Mae from her job as a secretary at AT&T that my dad had helped her find. Their ailments were mysterious to me, and I'm not sure that they were ever accurately diagnosed, but they involved fatigue, aches, and nervousness. My grandmother was still living, but rarely got out of bed, and, although my mother spent a few mornings each week helping, these two sickly women were her primary caretakers. I was saving money for graduate school and because my mother knew there were certain heavier cleaning jobs they could no longer do, she brokered a deal for me to do some housework for them.

In their three-bedroom house, Aunt Mae had the master bedroom with the attached bath. Her daily habit was to sit on the toilet, read romance novels, and smoke cigarettes, leaving the bathroom tile covered in a brownish gray film that it was now my job to clean. Armed with cleaning spray, bucket and brush, and a change of clothes, I spent three hours one afternoon in a bleach and steam-infused fog, removing years of nicotine stains.

After cleaning the tiles, cleaning myself off as best I could, and changing into dry clothes, I walked out to the living room to collect my pay. Carrie, however, was eager to talk. She had been watching the news, which had featured a topic that had gotten her worked up.

I knew some conversation would be required, but that was a skill I had not yet mastered with older relatives who were usually more conservative than I was. I didn't often agree with their views, but I was still young enough to fear their disapproval, and I hadn't learned to politely disagree without revealing too much about myself. Plus, I felt awkward and unkempt; even though I'd changed clothes, I was reluctant to sit on their pristine sofa.

I stood awkwardly while Aunt Carrie launched into what had upset her.

"Did you hear about that young girl who got AIDS from her dentist?" she asked, scandalized.

"Yeah, I did. That's pretty scary." This was 1990, when AIDS was believed to primarily affect homosexuals and drug users, details about its transmission were not clear, and a diagnosis was basically a death sentence. The woman was Kimberly Bergalis, a 23-year-old from Florida.

"I think that's just outrageous! He knew he had it. What was he doing seeing patients? I think they should put all those people on an island with just each other so they can't infect innocent people."

"You mean like a leper colony? I don't think that's right," I said.

"But, Tina, that girl didn't do anything wrong! She was a virgin! She had her whole life ahead of her." My aunt seemed to be taking this case personally.

"But wouldn't she have to go to the island now, too?"

"Well, she's so sick, they don't think she'll live much longer." In fact, this young woman did die about six months later.

I didn't share Aunt Carrie's outrage, so the topic fizzled. Aunt Mae had been uncharacteristically quiet. She would be diagnosed with Alzheimer's Disease within a few years, and I suspect she was already experiencing some of its symptoms. We chatted a few minutes more, and Carrie paid me more than the agreed price because the job had taken me so long.

Later, though, I still wondered why she became so heated over this story.

"Is Aunt Carrie a virgin?" I asked my mother.

"I don't know," she said, surprised. "Why would you ask that?"

I asked, of course, because I wondered if Aunt Carrie identified with the young woman in the news story because she, too, would likely die a virgin, and she felt embittered by that missed experience.

But my mother's answer wasn't what I expected. What I expected was something like, "Of course she is! She never married." I took her acknowledgment of the gray area surrounding this question as a good sign, an indication that we could now talk to each other as adults. But on the other hand, given how close the women in her family had always been, I also thought two sisters would share news of a first sexual experience. If it had ever happened, she would probably know about it.

But maybe not. I had always sensed mild resentment between my mother and Carrie. Joanne had been younger, but she was big-boned and healthy. Carrie, slight and sickly, had been treated like the baby even after their youngest brother was born, three years after my mother. Likewise healthy and prone to plumpness as a child, I could relate to the jealousy that crept into some of my mother's stories about their childhood. Of the five children, it was always Carrie who received special treatment.

"If anybody else misbehaved, Mama would tell Daddy to whip them. But nobody whipped Carrie because she was Daddy's pet."

Aunt Carrie was small and sweet, ultimate female virtues in the eyes of many men. As a girl, she grew shy around new people, but she loved to dance. With her brother Joel, four years her senior, she jitterbugged to Bennie Goodman and Glen Miller. Joel christened her his favorite partner because she knew the moves, followed his timing, and was light enough for him to lift easily. At an age when most older brothers shunned younger siblings, Joel begged his parents to let him take his thirteen-year-old sister to a dance so they could show off their moves.

With the promise of constant supervision and an early return, Joel took Carrie to the dance. My mother remembers them returning home, giddy with triumph.

"They cleared the dance floor for us," Joel boasted. "Everyone made a circle and just watched us."

This early conquest cemented Carrie's love of dancing, and she indulged whenever she found a partner, at high school dances, dinner-dance clubs, and community centers. In adulthood, as her peers married each other, partners were harder to find, but I remember seeing Carrie execute a subdued swing dance with her nephew at a family Christmas Eve party when I was a teen. She didn't look hokey, like a parody of someone dancing, the way my parents did. At once practiced and effortless, her feet, hips, and arms swayed in rhythmic harmony.

Even years later, in her final months at a nursing home, the staff told my mother that Carrie rose from her wheelchair for a brief waltz with the activity director, enjoying for the last time the glide of her body to music.

Carrie had been beautiful in her twenties. In an old photo album, my mother has a snapshot of her posed on a beach blanket in a black 1950s style one-piece bathing suit. This black-and-white photo shows sand and a few stray limbs of other beach-goers in the background, but Carrie is its sole focus. She sits reclining her weight against her arms, her breasts thrusting forward in the torpedo-shaped structure of the suit, her waist narrowing to an hourglass pinch, her legs curving mermaid-like before her. Her dark hair frames her face in waves, and she smiles radiantly at the camera like a pin-up girl.

In addition to being small and sweet, Carrie was prone to colds, headaches, and "female troubles." From the beginning, she suffered extremely heavy, painful periods. Some months it was so bad that her family feared for her safety; at those times, her father carried her wrapped in blankets to his pickup truck and drove her to the hospital for an injection to decrease the flow.

Doctors thought the problem would improve as she matured, but it didn't. Eventually they decided that uterine fibroids caused this heavy bleeding, and her doctor recommended a hysterectomy.

Given Carrie's symptoms and her age when they began, it's likely that she actually suffered from endometriosis, a disease that was known at the time but hard to diagnose and to treat. The difficulties with diagnosis and treatment were exacerbated, of course, by the tendency of male doctors to dismiss women's complaints about reproductive issues. At earlier times, western culture associated severe menstrual pain and heavy bleeding with everything from demonic possession to hysteria to nymphomania. By Carrie's day, the complaints were often dismissed as attention-seeking hypochondria. When a doctor diagnosed endometriosis, the only treatments available, short of hysterectomy, were medication for the pain or high doses of testosterone or estrogen, which had limited benefits and negative side effects. Today, doctors treat the disease more effectively with hormones in the form of birth control pills or IUDs and can even surgically remove the associated lesions, in some cases.

Growing up, Carrie had always assumed she'd one day marry and have children. The alternative, in her eyes, was to be an old maid, a fate that shouted a woman's undesirability or unworthiness, her failure, to the world. Partly because of her sickliness and partly because of her gender, she had been trained to believe she needed a partner in life, just as she did in a dance. Her parents taught her to fear venturing out at night or far from home without a trusted male attendant, a brother or a boy from a nice family, to ensure her safety.

Even in my youth, this attitude persisted. My father forbade evening outings with other girls. These were too dangerous. But a date with a trusted boyfriend, someone he had met and approved, was acceptable.

"Why do I need a boy there?" I asked him.

"To protect you. To let other men know that you're not available."

Apparently, seducers and rapists lurked around every corner. When my older sister moved out of the house and into her own apartment at age twenty-one, my father stalked her, calling her at 2 a.m. to make sure she was home. She even suspected him of stealing the license plate from her boyfriend's car when it was parked in front of her building overnight.

On some level, I must have believed my father, believed I was incapable of taking care of myself. This attitude helps to explain why I, in my efforts to free myself from his control, married for the first time at age nineteen.

But when Carrie protested the potential loss of a partner and children to her doctor, he reminded her that marriage was still available to her but children may not be possible even without the surgery. More immediately, the continued bleeding imperiled her health.

"Don't make more of it than it is," the doctor said. "I've just been comforting a woman whose baby was born dead. Your situation is nothing compared to hers."

The tone of this remembered conversation suggests the doctor's frustration at his patient's lingering symptoms, his dismissiveness of her concerns, and perhaps his unwillingness to try the less drastic alternatives of pain management and hormones.

At twenty-seven, Carrie went through with the operation, and then made sure she never saw that doctor again.

But she did have a brief stint at motherhood. Before I was born, Carrie and Mae helped raise two of my older cousins. These boys, Joel's sons, felt unwanted in their home after their mother ran off and their father remarried. Joel and Barbara wed in their teens and had the two children before she turned twenty. One day, when the boys were about two and four, Barbara packed a bag, took the boys to their grandmother, and left town on a bus. The children heard nothing from their mother for nearly twenty years; then she placed a call to the older one, who told her not to call again.

Within a year or two of her leaving, Joel remarried and had a child with his new wife. Justly or not, the boys felt neglected by their stepmother and successfully lobbied my grandmother and aunts to take them in. In their household, Aunt Mae made the rules and doled out discipline, and Aunt Carrie and my grandmother provided nurture and comfort. This arrangement lasted a few years until the family negotiated a new relationship and the boys moved back home to their father and stepmother.

Ironically, about five years after the day I cleaned the shower, the younger of the nephews Carrie helped raise also died of AIDS, which he contracted through unsafe sex or drug use. When he learned of his diagnosis, he drove from his home in Charlotte to tell his two aunts. His father had already died of cancer, so they were the closest things to parents he had left. From what I heard about this conversation later, Carrie accepted his news with sadness and love rather than judgment and condemnation. I wondered if she had already adjusted her perspective on this illness as public knowledge of it grew, or if she had been forced to swallow her prejudices whole when her prodigal nephew shared his story.

Aunt Carrie's motherly deeds extended to me when she chose my name. I was the third of my mother's children, and Carrie asked if she could name me. Maybe my mother was out of ideas, or maybe she felt sorry for her sister, 36 and childless. Carrie had heard the name Betina in a movie or TV show, and thought it sounded elegant. Perhaps it was "The Bettina May Story" episode of the Wagon Train series that aired in 1961 and starred Bette Davis as the titular frontier widow and matriarch. This was the name she gave me, although my family spelled it with one "t," and I have always gone by Tina.

When I was a child, when she was in her forties, I thought Carrie was still beautiful. I'd occasionally see her in her neat, white dental assistant uniform, sporting a competent and friendly air. She was the aunt who pulled me to her lap on Christmas Eve to ask what Santa Claus was going to bring me or allowed me to cuddle next to her on a chair while the adults talked after a family dinner. When we visited her house on Sundays, she was the one who offered me a Coke and a dish of homemade banana pudding or coconut layer cake.

Carrie also had a soft heart. She donated money to a charity that provided scholarships for Native Americans because, she said, "This country has given them a raw deal." Even though she knew no Native Americans personally, she romanticized their culture and mourned its devastation. She would have liked to travel to other parts of the country to visit their territory, but didn't feel safe traveling alone. The furthest she'd ever been from home was a trip to Raleigh, NC with Mae and my grandmother to visit one of her nephews.

But as Aunt Carrie aged and her health became even more fragile, her looks and sweetness faded and she grew irritable with pain and fatigue. When Carrie carped at Joanne, I sensed her smoldering jealousy of my mother as counterpart to the lingering hints of resentment Joanne felt for Carrie. Sometimes she criticized Joanne's housekeeping skills. Because she and Mae lived in a household of adult women, their home, even when they worked full-time jobs, was spotless, at least until they got too old and sick to clean it. Joanne's home, with four kids, was not.

"Look at this dishwasher door! You're home all day, Joanne. Why don't you clean this? I'd be ashamed!" In response, my mother would laugh a little, acknowledge that she was right and move on to something else. Later, she'd share these remarks with me, starting with an exasperated, "Do you know what she said?"

As she aged, Aunt Carrie got even thinner, but my mother, who had always struggled with her weight, saw the pounds piling on throughout her 40s and 50s. This, too, was a target of criticism.

"A grown woman doesn't need more than a half sandwich at lunchtime, Joanne! You're just going to have to learn to say no. Men and growing children need more, but you can't eat like they do."

So, when my mother didn't know if Carrie was a virgin, I thought of this history and wondered if they were as close as I had assumed.

"She was engaged twice, but she never talked about that sort of thing with me," my mother said.

"She was?" I asked. "Who was she engaged to?"

"She was engaged to the dentist she worked for when she was in her 40s, but it didn't work out."

Now that she mentioned it, I did remember the stunning diamond ring she had worn for a time with her white pantsuit uniform. I also remembered that the young woman from the news story had been infected by her dentist. I briefly imagined the ex-fiancé had been a philandering predator, and that Carrie's outrage at the girl's fate had been prompted by her memories of Dr. Boss's mistreatment of her.

"I don't remember the details, but I think Carrie broke it off after an argument because she thought he was trying to control her," my mother said. "He was twenty years older, and I think she thought of him as a father figure. They started dating not long after Daddy died.

"She was also engaged to another boy named Ronnie when she was younger, but that didn't work out either."

"What happened that time?"

"She broke up with him, but she never said why."

So, my initial question remained unanswered, and I was left to assume what is likely true: that my aunt, also a virgin who hadn't done anything wrong, felt outraged for Kimberly Bergalis who faced a fate that was even more unfair than Carrie's. Of course, it was more than just the sex they'd both missed out on. To my aunt and to Miss Bergalis, sex meant marriage. And to my Aunt, at least, marriage meant a steady partner for other pursuits, such as dancing and traveling, in which a lone woman should not indulge.

It was only later that I knew there was yet a deeper layer to fate's unfair dealings with Carrie and that my mother, at least in her own eyes, may have played a part in brokering the bad deal.

When Carrie was in her early twenties, she and Ronnie dated for a time and then broke up. Shortly after this, Joanne, about 19 then, received a letter from Ronnie, which she promptly shared with her two older sisters.

"I've always thought you were very nice and pretty and I'd like to take you out," the letter said. "But we'd have to meet somewhere. I don't want to come to your house just now because of Carrie."

Ronnie requested a reply, and Carrie and Mae helped Joanne write one.

At their dictation, she wrote, "I'm sorry, but my sisters and I are not in the habit of dating each other's discarded boyfriends."

Joanne thought Ronnie's letter was inappropriate, but she also felt the reply was a little mean. She sent it anyway. Later, Joanne ran into Ronnie while out with other young people and smoothed over hurt feelings. I'm not sure if my mother ever went on a date with Ronnie. I know she never dated him seriously, but she must have had at least one serious conversation with him.

As I mentioned, in 1954, just two weeks shy of her 21st birthday, Joanne married my father. Ronnie hadn't given up on the family, however.

Several years later Carrie and Ronnie got back together and their relationship grew serious. In late 1959, when Carrie was 29 years old, Ronnie proposed marriage and she accepted.

That was a good Christmas for the family. Joanne had just had her first child, my older brother, in November, and Carrie was beginning her wedding plans.

Here's the part I learned only recently, that my mother kept to herself back in 1990.

I picture them sitting at Carrie's kitchen table with cups of coffee, my infant brother sleeping in my mother's arms. They probably talked about wedding plans: a wedding at Kilbourne Park Baptist Church, a small reception at the church's fellowship hall, Mae as maid of honor and Joanne as matron of honor.

Shifting the baby in her arms, my mother asked, "Did you tell Ronnie you can't have children?"

"No," Aunt Carrie answered. "It hasn't come up."

"Well, I think you should. I know he really wants a family. He told me that years ago." At this point I imagine Carrie would have changed the subject, stood and taken the dishes to the sink.

"The next thing I heard about it, the wedding was off," my mother told me recently. "She would never talk about what happened, at least not that I ever heard. I felt bad about it, if what I said was the reason they broke up. But he had a right to know."

Of course, she's right. For all she knows, though, Carrie may have never told him. The breakup could have been over something else, or she may have ended things preemptively before he had a chance to reject her. But I also wonder if my mother, on some level, felt a small satisfaction in besting the prettier, petted sister.

Regardless of why it happened, without a partner, Carrie never allowed herself to dance.

After I moved on to graduate school and then to my first college teaching job, I didn't see my aunts often. My grandmother died a few years after the day I cleaned the shower, and Aunt Mae went to a memory care facility about five years after that.

After Aunt Mae's death, my mother helped Carrie sort through Mae's clothes, jewelry, and other personal items. Some they kept, some they gave to other family members, and some they donated. Doing this chore would make anyone feel retrospective, but especially two sisters sifting through the accumulated belongings of someone they'd known their whole lives. Carrie was about 75 then, and she had already experienced a qualified win against cancer of the lymph nodes, qualified because the cancer-destroying radiation had damaged her heart.

Sitting on her sister's old taupe sateen bedspread, surrounded by furniture bearing cologne, face powder, and hairspray that would never be used again, black and white photos of long-dead relatives, and yellowed slips and bras spilling from drawers, Carrie uttered one of the most heartbreaking sentences I've ever heard.

"Joanne, when I think about what I've done with my life, I could just cry."

— 7 —

Tammy, Tea Parties,
and the Telephone

I learned from Aunt Ella that grief doesn't kill, at least not quickly, but when it lasts for thirty years, its cumulative power can certainly be deadly. My cousin Tammy suffered a fatal heart attack in 2018, at the age of fifty-two. Her adult life was plagued by anxiety, depression, substance abuse, and unending mourning. Although she was once my closest friend, throughout adulthood, I barely knew her.

Tammy was my best friend from the time I started making friends until the end of middle school. She had a swimming pool in her backyard, not a cheap above-ground pool that you can buy for $499 at Wal-Mart, but a beautiful in-ground pool with a diving board and a slide. For this reason, I believed as a child that her family was better than mine. Her father, my mother's brother, was a middle manager at the phone company, and her mother worked, too. They had more money than we did, even though my father claimed to have gotten my uncle his first real job.

I loved swimming in Tammy's pool. When our siblings were there, we all played Marco Polo or had chicken fights, but when Tammy and I swam alone, we often had underwater tea parties. Tammy's mother, Aunt Eva, sat in her modest one-piece bathing suit in a lounge chair by the pool, cigarette in one hand and a cold drink, which I always thought was spiked, in the other. Her short black hair had a few strands of gray, and her skin was tanned and leathery. Since Tammy swam expertly, but I had mastered only a floundering dog paddle, I'm sure my aunt was there mainly to keep an eye on me.

Our underwater tea parties began with a surface dive. Tammy looked like a seal doing this maneuver. She bent gracefully at the waist, ducked her head below the water—her long, dark hair floating behind her—and flipped her feet up into the air as she dove for the bottom of the pool. After trying and failing at this, I usually reached the bottom by simply sitting, aiding gravity by paddling my hands. Although both of us were chubby and frequently awkward at nine and ten, Tammy achieved a grace in the water that eluded me.

Resting on the bottom of the pool, we pantomimed serving and drinking tea, pouring from an invisible pot into dainty, invisible cups, from which we drank like ladies. The necessity of holding our breath added an element of competition to this game, and once again, Tammy was much better than I.

With the chlorine burning my eyes and the lack of oxygen burning my lungs, I burst to the surface after one brief fake sip from my cup, gulping air while Tammy lounged below. Finally appearing above water, Tammy gloated silently and said we should play again, but after a few rounds of the tea party game, Aunt Eva told us to play something else, probably fearing I would drown.

To my child's eyes, Tammy's family was better than mine for other reasons as well. She and I frequently slept over at each other's houses on weekends, and her parents were more indulgent and permissive than mine. They bought Tammy a moped when she was twelve, and we rode it, her driving and me holding on behind, to the nearby shopping center and all around her neighborhood. On one of these excursions, I borrowed Tammy's lip gloss, applied it using a drug store mirror, and then glanced at the surveillance camera in the ceiling as Tammy placed the lip gloss back in her purse. We were able to explain the situation—we had not in fact been shoplifting—to the stocky, uniformed black woman with a gold-edged tooth who appeared seconds later, but she warned us to "be cool" in the future.

Another favorite pastime was prank phone calls, always from Tammy's house, because I feared being caught at mine.

"I'm from the power company and I'm conducting a survey. Is your refrigerator running?" Tammy would ask. "Then you'd better catch it before it gets away!"

We both burst into laughter, and Tammy hung up the phone.

Once I asked Tammy which house she preferred for sleepovers.

"Mine," she replied.

"Me, too," I agreed. "There's more to do at your house."

"Plus, it's too hot at your house."

While Tammy's house had central air conditioning, mine was cooled by window units that my father would turn on only if the forecast predicted a high of ninety-five degrees or more. On summer nights, the heat stifled us and thwarted sleep. An attic fan drew in warm air from the outside, but we were only permitted to open the windows two inches because my father believed this narrow gap led to more forceful airflow and a cooler house.

"It's physics," he explained. I think he also feared that wide-open windows would invite intruders to slit the screens and climb inside.

One particularly hot night when Tammy slept over, after she believed everyone else was asleep, she rose from bed and tiptoed to the window. Just as she tried to lift the stiff sash, my father appeared in the bedroom doorway.

"Don't touch that," he ordered.

Tammy, about twelve then, replied, "But it's hot as hell in here! I'm just trying to open the window."

"Leave it alone and get back to bed. The fan is on."

"Well, it's not doing a very good job," she sulked.

"You're a spoiled brat. Get to bed and stay there!" I was hot too, and I had been rooting for Tammy as she challenged my father. But I also inwardly balked at the way she thought she could defy the rules so easily. If it were that simple, I would already have done it.

Tammy and I used to talk on the phone for an hour or more, several afternoons a week, and as I mentioned earlier, she clued me in on family gossip in some of these conversations. But just recently, I learned that one time, shortly after the window incident, she called my father.

"I've talked it over with Mama and Daddy, and we think that Tina should come live here with us," she said. "You keep it too hot over there, and she'd be better off here."

When my father asked to speak to Tammy's parents, she hung up. He promptly called back and got them, but they, of course, knew nothing about this proposed change to my living arrangements. She was grounded, and we didn't see each other for a few weeks, but my father never mentioned the phone call to me or, surprisingly, to my mother. Tammy's older sister, Erin, told me about it after her funeral.

I saw my first concert—Sean Cassidy—with Tammy and Aunt Eva. Another time, my aunt treated my cousin and me to a week-long vacation at Myrtle Beach. She booked an efficiency motel room near the boardwalk and gave us far more independence than my parents would have, reading novels and tanning while we swam and giggled at boys. I remember standing in the second floor, open-air motel corridor one night while Aunt Eva watched TV in the room. Tammy dared me to talk to two older boys on the sidewalk below, so I yelled "Hey guys!" over the railing.

To our surprise and horror, they turned and walked toward the motel's stairway.

"You're not coming up here, are you?" I asked.

"We're just coming up to say hello."

We had both matured early and used too much makeup; that night I wore a black tank top and white shorts, and Tammy wore a tight t-shirt. Evidently these boys in their late teens or early twenties thought we were older than our actual ages of twelve and thirteen. When they reached the second floor and saw us up close, they chatted a few minutes and left. Tammy and I bought sodas from the vending machine and returned to our room, chastened.

As we grew into our teen years, though, Tammy and I drifted apart. We lived on opposite ends of town and went to different schools. Tammy's school friends, upper-middle-class preppies, wore Izod shirts, Ralph Lauren jeans, and Sperry

Top-Sider shoes, while my friends were an eclectic mix of freaks and geeks. She listened to Donna Summer or Earth, Wind & Fire, but I preferred Led Zeppelin or Lynyrd Skynyrd. When she spoke of my clothes, my music, or my friends, I sometimes heard her sneer.

When I was fourteen, I made the mistake of confiding in her about my boyfriend, Kevin, whom I loved with all the passion of a thwarted teenage romance.

Before the night of the party when Kevin and I had sex together, on the phone with Tammy, I tearfully declared my love for him and bemoaned that he hadn't called in a week. Because he told me so, I knew he wanted a girlfriend he could have sex with, and I fantasized aloud about running away from home to do this.

"Gross! You're fourteen!" Tammy said. "You shouldn't do that until you're married."

I was in no mood to listen to this type of reasoning, and Tammy soon ended our one-sided conversation. A few weeks later, having no one else to confide in, I told her all about the consummation of our relationship in a furtive phone call when my parents weren't around. Her voice revealed scornful amusement and disapproval; I could hear it even then. But because my emotional isolation felt so complete at the time, and because the action had symbolized in part my bid at self-definition, the act of telling it made it more real and enduring, placing my rough-draft of a self out in the world.

Days later, after school, the phone rang and, as always, I ran to answer before anyone else had the chance.

"Hello, Tina. This is Kevin." It was my cousin's voice, unconvincingly deepened to sound like a boy.

"Tammy, I know it's you," I said. A room full of her friends burst into laughter before she hung up.

Tammy's betrayal compounded Kevin's (by this time, he had broken up with me for good) and deepened my humiliation. She made a similar call a few days later, and that ended our friendship. After this, I saw Tammy at infrequent family gatherings, and we never talked about her prank calls. We were polite to each other but guarded. We swam in different circles now.

Late in my high school years, my mother told me one spring day that Aunt Eva had been hospitalized. Her kidneys were failing and she began regular dialysis.

I should have called Tammy then, but I didn't. I had a part-time job, a new boyfriend, and I had become a serious student. All of these things absorbed my time, but, more importantly, resentment still dominated my emotions.

I saw Tammy and Aunt Eva once a year now, at the family Christmas Eve party they hosted for near and distant relatives and their family's close friends. A few months after Eva's hospitalization, they held the party as usual.

"I need a cigarette," said Tammy. "Do you want to come to my room and have one with me?"

"Okay," I said. But in the bedroom, I asked, "Won't your parents get mad at you for smoking?"

"Mama doesn't care. She bums cigarettes from me when she runs out." Neither of us spoke about Aunt Eva's illness, but behind Tammy's eyes I saw fragility and sadness, as if the failure to forbid smoking were a symptom of her mother's physical decline.

By the next Christmas Eve, we had both started college, and Tammy's family had moved to a new, more impressive lake house. I attended that year's gathering with my fiancé, and the year after that, we attended as husband and wife. I spoke to Tammy only briefly, but her close friends were there to keep her company. Each year, Aunt Eva grew thinner and frailer, chatting cheerfully from a chair instead of bustling among the guests.

In my third year of college, Tammy's fourth, Aunt Eva called my mother to say they wouldn't be having their Christmas Eve gathering. She'd just had another stint in the hospital and was too weak to pull it all together. My mother decided to have a more intimate version of the party at our house, inviting her four siblings and their families. But despite the decorations, the Christmas music, and half a dozen different desserts, our party was not as festive as Aunt Eva's.

The subdued atmosphere was due partly to the smaller number of guests and partly to the limited drink selection. Whereas Aunt Eva's parties featured a fully stocked bar, ours offered only lime punch or sweet, pink wine, the kind favored by high school girls who pool their money and cajole an older sibling into buying them alcohol. More importantly, though, everyone's mood suffered because we feared Aunt Eva's parties were forever lost.

Tammy's family arrived a little late, and my uncle helped Aunt Eva to a chair in the living room, where most of the older relatives sat. She was thinner and paler than before and stooped at the shoulders as if she were too weak to stand up straight. Mother brought her a plate, while my uncle and cousins helped themselves.

The younger family members congregated in the den, where the conversation was a little freer.

"How is your mom doing?" my older sister asked.

"She's okay. She's getting around better today," Erin replied. "They gave her a colostomy bag in the hospital," she added. "It's the funniest thing. Sometimes she'll be talking, or watching TV, or just sitting there quiet, and ppffftttt! You can hear it across the room!" Erin laughed, coping with her worry through humor. The rest of us laughed, too, uncomfortably, and I saw fear in Tammy's eyes.

Today, I can still picture those eyes: deep brown, large, and furtive, refusing to hold my gaze. And I can hear her tentative laughter that came with a shaky, brief smile. Tammy was tall, about six feet, and at this point in her life she was thinner than she ever would be again, although still big-boned and fleshy. Her long black hair waved gently around her winter-pale, attractive face. She always dressed in expensive, fashionable clothes, but she seemed uneasy in them, as if she wished she could shrink three sizes. Because I kept that memory, I must have still cared deeply for her, or at least for the memory of the two of us as children. I've always been guarded about exposing my feelings, and at that time, I was still wary of Tammy. She and Erin were too quick to laugh at others' flaws, and even if they intended it affectionately, I disliked being vulnerable. I don't recall saying much that night, but the anxiety I glimpsed in Tammy became a recurring theme in her life.

Aunt Eva couldn't smoke in our house, and she needed her rest, so they only stayed about ninety minutes. Her parties usually lasted until after midnight, but ours broke up much earlier, leaving me, and probably our guests, feeling let down.

+ + +

Months later, as the azaleas and dogwoods bloomed, Aunt Eva died. She was in her mid-fifties. I cried when my mother told me, but not until after I'd hung up the phone. The pain took a few minutes to surface, like when a child skins her knee and only cries when the sight of blood confirms she's hurt. I didn't go to the funeral, though, having the true but inadequate justification of having classes to attend, papers to write, and my part-time job at the mall lingerie store. "You don't need to go," mother said on the phone. "We'll be there." But today, far too late to rectify or apologize, guilt stalks me for failing to pay my respects.

My mother and her sisters helped Erin and Tammy sort through their mother's belongings a few months after the funeral. The girls kept what they wanted, but most of her clothes were given away.

"Do you want to come look at some of these things?" my mother asked. "She had some nice pieces that were barely worn, and they look like they're about your size."

My husband and I were newly separated, and I had refused to move back home. I was an impoverished student, living on my college scholarship and minimum wage from the lingerie store, and my mother knew I couldn't afford to buy clothes.

I ended up keeping several of the pieces my mother brought home with her, and there's one that I can still visualize today. The matching full skirt and boat-necked, three-quarter sleeved blouse looked like a dress when you wore them together. Horizontal pinstripes of orange, white, green, and yellow crossed the black, synthetic fabric. I needed to dress up for my job, so this outfit became a part of my regular fall rotation.

As it turned out, I was wearing it the next time I saw Tammy. It was near Christmas, school was out, and I was working extra hours at the lingerie store. Walking through the mall before work, I saw Tammy a few yards away, in the midst of her Christmas shopping. Carols played on the sound system, and a Salvation Army Santa rang a bell. Garland, holly, poinsettia, and fake snow decorated the mall planters and shop windows. For a second I froze, wishing I had worn something different that day and wondering if I could flee in the other direction without being seen.

At that moment, Tammy looked up, said hello, and closed the distance between us.

"Are you Christmas shopping?"

"Heading to work," I replied, pointing to the store.

"I love that store. They have such pretty things."

"Yeah, I love to look at it, but I can't really buy any of it," I said.

As we stood in the tiled mall corridor, chatting politely, I hoped Tammy wouldn't recognize her mother's dress. I kept my face neutral and my gaze steady, willing myself not to look down at my clothes.

"How are you doing?" I asked.

"Doing okay. I'm finishing up school this year. I'm on the five-year plan," she said breezily.

Neither of us spoke about Aunt Eva, even though this was her time of year—the annual party, the only time I saw

Tammy. Grief for her mother had hit Tammy especially hard, I'd heard, and it was the first Christmas since her death. She had liked to party at college, but coping with her mother's final illness prompted her to drink even more. Her drinking and depression led her to fail several classes. All of this ran through my mind, but I kept it submerged.

In the almost thirty years that followed this day, Tammy continued to self-medicate with alcohol, eventually in combination with her prescription Paxil. I kept up with her on social media, where she frequently shared posts about mental health awareness and suicide prevention, as well as nostalgic remembrances of her mother. She eventually married and had a son, about the same age as my son. I stopped by their house one summer when I visited Columbia and found them all in the backyard by the pool. While her husband and son played in the water, Tammy sat on the steps in the shallow end with a bottle of wine. She offered me a glass and cheerily announced that this was her second bottle of the afternoon. At occasional family gatherings where I saw them, Erin chided Tammy for her love of wine, at first good-naturedly and then, when Tammy developed diabetes, with more fervor. She and I had grown too far apart for intimate conversations, so I never commented on her excesses.

But why wasn't I able to offer her some comfort that day in the mall? I'm still not sure. At the time, it happened so fast, but with the luxury of decades to look back on that moment, I see Tammy as a sad, motherless girl whom I long to embrace.

But again, it's far too late for that.

That day in the mall, the air felt thick with all we didn't say. For a minute, I thought maybe it was just me; maybe

Tammy hadn't noticed the dress, maybe she didn't suffer this awkwardness. But then I saw tears gathering in her eyes, and I realized we were both pretending.

"This is your last year, too, right?" Tammy asked casually.

"Yeah. Just one semester to go."

I thought of the underwater tea parties from long ago, as if we were politely holding our breaths again, each of us refusing to acknowledge that I wore her dead mother's hand-me-down clothes. I wanted to say, "I'm sorry."

But this time, it was Tammy who burst to the surface first.

"Well, Merry Christmas," she said, turning her face just as the first tears slipped down her cheeks and hurrying past the mall's artificial cheer.

— 8 —

Flood House

My town of Bloomsburg, Pennsylvania, sits nestled at the intersection of the wide brown waters of the Susquehanna River, and the long and winding but not-so-wide Fishing Creek. Many parts of town are prone to flooding, and I owned a house in one of those areas during my most recent marriage.

Living through a major flood and living through the end of a marriage have much in common. A gradual accumulation of bad decisions, neglect, and uncontrollable external forces make each disaster possible. Then, once the flood or the end of the marriage actually starts, it happens quickly, often before we have time to minimize the damage. In both cases, the aftermath, the cleanup, is the hardest part.

When I bought my sturdy, one-hundred-year-old house across the street from Fishing Creek in 2005, the previous owner told me that the only flooding she had ever experienced was an inch or two in the basement during Hurricane Agnes in 1972, a flood still legendary among older residents of the region. It needed some work but had good bones, with two stories, three bedrooms, one and a half baths, hardwood floors, a bonus room, a wide front porch, and a large backyard. At age thirty-eight, I moved in with my new husband Joe, our newborn son Cody, my four-year-old child from my third marriage, Blair (who also lived half-time with their father), and with the somehow-still-naive belief that this house, this marriage would be different than the ones before.

This wasn't my first flood house. But I left the previous house, where I had lived with Blair's father, before it had a chance to flood. We had been married for about three years, and Blair, a wispy pixie of a child, was not quite two. I was thirty-four and working toward tenure at the university, focusing too much on my career while my husband focused too much on our child. Blair, for example, had never slept in their own bed because their father couldn't stand to hear them cry. I didn't ignore my child, but I did ignore my husband, and Blair definitely had a closer relationship with him than he had with me.

When I eventually had a brief affair with a married colleague, our marriage completed its collapse, like a condemned building that instantly and totally implodes after the charges have been painstakingly laid. My colleague and I didn't exactly keep our affair a secret; we were both unconsciously seeking a way out of unhappy relationships, although my partner in crime eventually found a way to renegotiate his and save the marriage.

In part, this is a story of past trauma leading to future dysfunction: when my husband found out about our affair, he hacked my email and suspiciously monitored my phone. In an angry confrontation with him, the thought that entered my head, which should have raised all sorts of red flags, was: "I'm an adult! You can't tell me who I can and cannot see."

This was the voice of adolescent Tina addressing her father. My thwarted affair had merged with my frustrated romance with Kevin, then twenty years in the past. Just as I had defiantly consummated my eighth-grade love, and damn the consequences, I had pursued an extramarital liaison that had little chance of going undetected. In both cases, I intended to send a signal.

Although the marriage fell apart, we managed to co-parent Blair amicably and cooperatively, and I believe my relationship with my child actually improved. I did seek counseling, though not yet quite enough. My ex-husband continued to live in our former house, and when the creek rose four years later, he had to deal with that mostly himself.

In 2005, I optimistically embarked on a new marriage in a new flood house. The following year, drought followed by torrential rains and late snowmelt led to record flooding. As the creek across the street neared its bank that afternoon, township police officers walked the neighborhood, knocking on doors, warning residents that a flood was predicted, and encouraging everyone to evacuate. We lived on the high side of the street. Our house sat on a hill about eight feet above the level of the road in front, and the road and houses across the street sat about nine feet above the normal level of the creek. Joe and I stood on our porch, looked at Fishing Creek, and decided there was no way the water could reach us.

By the next morning, the rain had stopped, but the water continued to rise. It was level with the bank in front of our house now, at the bottom of the porch steps, making our street a temporary river. But the house's foundation lifted the first floor another five feet, so only our basement had flooded so far. Three feet of water stood in the basement, and Joe and I realized with fright that the electricity was still on and the water would soon reach the breaker box. As I stood nervously at the top of the basement steps, Joe turned on a flashlight and went down into the murky brown water, pushing aside floating toys and household items, until he reached the box. With a wooden broom handle, he flipped the main breaker without being electrocuted.

Later that day, at the flood's peak, I stood on the front porch with five-year-old Blair and one-year-old Cody. A helicopter beat the air over the neighborhood, televising the damage for viewers and looking for stranded residents. The floodwaters were easily six feet deep on the street before our house, the current swift enough to propel hot tubs and sofas past. I was awed by the water's power and reach, amazed that it had risen this high, but I was still not worried for our safety. The backyard sloped upward to the neighbor's yard and, beyond that, a higher street, so I knew we had an escape route.

A game of "What will the floodwaters bring?" entertained Blair for at least an hour. We had no electricity for TV or videos, so I was thankful for the distraction. Although water flooded only our basement, the houses across the street, on the low side, were submerged to the middle of their first-floor windows. These folks had sensibly evacuated.

Within a day or two, the water had subsided, and the heartbreaking work of cleanup began. Neighbors helped one another shovel stinking mud, hurl soggy carpets and furniture into dumpsters, rip out drywall, spray everything down with a mixture of bleach and water to prevent mold, and begin to rebuild. Neighborhoods not affected by the flood brought in donations of bottled water and food. The cleanup took weeks, and rebuilding took much longer.

Everyone talked about the flood for years after, labeling it a one-hundred-year flood. We had lived through a historic event. Blair liked to remind me of how many hot tubs floated past our house (two), and Cody complained that he was too young to remember it.

In Bloomsburg, as in other places throughout the country, neglect and bad decisions have led to conditions that make flooding more frequent and severe. Added to the global problems of climate change are the local problems, including the 2002 development of a shopping plaza with 200 acres of impermeable asphalt, and the failure to dredge the accumulation of human-created debris from the creek and river. But most people are slow to link cause and effect.

Neglect and bad decisions also created the conditions that led to my fourth divorce. This marriage didn't suddenly end when my husband found a girlfriend, as I implied earlier. When the first flood hit, we had only been married about a year. We weathered it well, almost like an adventure, and we also looked forward to renovations inside the house, even though the first and second floors had not been damaged.

Yet many would think our marriage was ill-advised. He was thirteen years younger than me, a former student of mine, whom I began dating after his graduation. For the record, he pursued me, at least at first. Joe looked older than his actual years, with flecks of early gray in his dark-brown hair and slight wrinkles caused by smoking and the worries of a difficult childhood. In turn, I looked a little younger than my years due to a healthy diet and exercise and a lucky draw from the gene pool. In 2007, he was a twenty-seven-year-old middle-school teacher, father, stepfather, husband, and homeowner who had survived a flood. I was a forty-year-old triple divorcée with children from two marriages, headed for a flood of karmic misery.

Gradually, as a few years passed, each of us began to neglect aspects of our marriage. I am a morning person, so I rose early to grade papers or prepare for class, but Joe, a night owl, worked late into the evening, and most nights, we had different sleeping schedules. The sex was good, but he wanted more of it than I did—that is, until he grew bored with the monotony. He coached high school basketball, and I, never a sports enthusiast, resented—vocally—this time away from me and the children. I was writing a book of literary criticism, and he tired of my single-minded attention to this task that would yield small rewards and an even smaller audience.

I know this type of distance occurs in many marriages over time. Recently, a secretary at work celebrated her thirtieth wedding anniversary, for which her husband ordered a large floral arrangement to be delivered to the office. I asked her how they had stayed together so long, but she revealed no magic formula.

"He watches TV downstairs, and I watch TV upstairs," she said. "After a while, you figure, what's the point in changing things."

I hope the secret to a lasting marriage is more than just inertia, but I'll never know. I will never marry again, and my boyfriend and I won't live together until after both my children have left for college.

Sometime during this period, Kevin contacted me on Facebook, an act that I read in hindsight as symbolically significant, as I do most things. By this time, more than thirty years had passed since I knew him, but when I got the friend request, I instantly remembered. As a middle-aged man, he looked like a refugee from the movie Easy Rider, complete with a motorcycle. And although his life's path could not have been more different from mine—high school GED followed by a career in the military, from which he'd recently retired (yet, similarly, four marriages)—I began to fantasize about a do-over to our romance. As I said, I had not yet had enough counseling, but this time, I did see those red flags waving in the distance.

Our catching up was short-lived, lasting only a few weeks, and we conducted it solely over instant messenger. There were no plans to meet or even talk on the phone. Yet I felt guilty, and one evening, on Valentine's Day no less, after too much wine, I told Joe all about it.

The depth of his resentment surprised me, and a few days later, when we discussed it further, he astutely cried, "You're not a teenager anymore!"

Joe asked to read our correspondence, so I logged into my Facebook account for him and left the room. What stuck with him were Kevin's comments: "I never forgot you" and "You still look great," kind words that someone might say at a high school reunion.

Another lesson in past trauma that leads to future dysfunction: about a week later, when Joe said, "I don't want to fight anymore. Let's just forget it," I thought everything was better, but of course it wasn't.

Then, about five years after the first flood, our town saw its second one-hundred-year flood, and this one was worse than the first. A tropical storm had stalled over the East Coast that September, and we were bombarded with heavy rains.

Late that afternoon, Joe called my office. "You better leave now," he said. "The water's almost to the road, and they aren't sure how long the bridge will be open."

I drove home through an inch of water on our street and parked the car as high as possible in the yard above our driveway. As neighbors evacuated across the street, we prepared to stay. This time, we remembered to shut off the electricity and carry valuables up from the basement.

"Looks like you'll get your chance to see another flood," I told Cody.

Before dawn, the water lapped on the top step, six inches below our front porch, while my children slept inside on the second floor. We still had an easy escape route out the back, but as I nervously begged the water to stop rising, I swore to myself that, next time, I would evacuate. As morning advanced, the water began to recede, and Joe and I breathed easier.

We now knew that labels like "one-hundred-year-flood" are unreliable; clearly something had changed. Many neighbors whose houses suffered heavy damage had no interest in rebuilding; they applied for and received buy-outs from the government. The homeowners received fair market value for their property, and the houses would be destroyed, leveled to grassy fields, to prevent future losses.

But once again, my house received comparatively little damage. We cleared out the basement, Joe throwing soggy items up the steps to me, me throwing them in the giant community dumpster that had been left across the street for flood cleanup. In both floods, the aspect of the cleanup that surprised me most was the smell. The mud reeked of fermented earth, rot, and the residue of gas and oil picked up by the waters. Joe shoveled inches of this mud and sprayed the basement walls with bleach and water. We helped our neighbors clear their debris, waited for the electricity and plumbing to be restored, and contacted the insurance company about a new furnace and water heater.

After this, I lived in fear of the next flood and wanted to sell, but Joe knew we would never get the house's previous value. I wanted to update the bonus room and the half bathroom with an eye to selling the next year, and he wanted to do the work himself, which would take much longer but save money. These new pressures distanced us further, and we thought the best way to lessen the strain was to avoid talking about it.

Joe retiled the floor in the bonus room, and I painted the walls a light green. When our friend came to the house for dinner a few days later, Joe showed him our work.

"Tina painted it. You can see a green spot on the ceiling there where she hit it with the roller."

Later that evening, Joe told our friend of his growing dissatisfaction at work. "I think I might teach a few more years and then maybe go into contracting instead."

This was the first I had heard of his unhappiness or his alternate career plan.

After a while, the tension between us began to affect the children as well. Once, when we planned a family game night, the children wanted to play two different games, so Blair suggested the two of us play together while Cody played with his dad.

"Blair always does that," Joe complained. "I don't know if it's intentional, but it divides our family." When I suggested we all play one game and then the other, Joe and Blair both complained.

Still, I thought we were just experiencing normal family disagreements, not the beginning of the end. Then, Joe and I began to fight about almost everything—chores, money, childrearing—and each time our voices grew loud, Cody cried and fled the room.

In November 2012, we both forgot our wedding anniversary, and around this time, I did see, finally, that the marriage was in trouble.

"What's going on?" I asked him one night in bed.

"I'm just really busy with school and basketball," he told me. "I'm feeling a lot of stress right now."

"You seem really unhappy. Is it about us?" I pushed.

"How come when you're stressed out, it's just stress, but when I'm stressed out, you think it's us?" His voice flared with exasperation, so I let it go.

Although the end began much earlier, the final blow came in February of 2013. There was a Saturday evening basketball game, and my husband told me on Friday night that he was calling an extra practice the next morning, something he hadn't done before. As I angrily complained about this extra time away from home, my seven-year-old son stuck up for his father.

"Mom, he has to do basketball!"

"Well, that doesn't mean he shouldn't spend time with you, does it?!" I yelled. Cody stood up from the sofa with tears in his eyes, walked out to the front porch, and slammed the door.

At that moment, I saw it happen. Joe didn't look at me or say anything, but his eyes narrowed as if he were tallying a column of numbers in his head; then, satisfied with the sum, he nodded so slightly I almost didn't see it and suggested we go out to dinner. Although I had no idea at the time, I later realized that he had been weighing me against his new romantic interest, the discord in our marriage against the discord of divorce. That weekend, after the game, he told me he wanted out.

◆ ◆ ◆

I wish I understood better why I, like so many of my ancestresses, have struggled so much in my pursuit of happiness. Am I a bad judge of men the way I'm a bad judge of houses? In the midst of the floods, I reassured myself that we always had an escape route out the back. Maybe that's the way I subconsciously think about marriage—there's always an escape route: divorce. Maybe I'm wary of feeling trapped, the way I perceived my mother to be, the way I felt as a teenager. But by resurrecting my ancestresses' voices, I quiet some of the internal voices that keep me sad, such as the inner harpy who pinpoints my failures and flaws, and the inner Fury who wants revenge. Telling these misfit women's stories allows me to make more sense of mine, to hear it and be okay.

✦ ✦ ✦

Within a month, Joe moved to an apartment, and when that dust settled, I knew I could no longer live in a flood house. The place had painful memories, and the stress of a flood and its aftermath were more than I could handle alone. I sold some AT&T stock my father had given me, paid my ex-husband for his share in the house, and started looking for a new home.

My children had different reactions to the idea of moving. Blair had a close relationship with their father and lived half of the time at his house. Perhaps for this reason, they had never closely bonded with their stepfather. To Blair, a new house meant simply a new place to live.

Cody had handled his father's move gracefully. He enjoyed staying at the new apartment and liked the one-on-one time with his dad. But when I broached the subject of selling our house, he grew sad and angry.

"I love this house!" he said. "All of my good memories are here." To him, this place represented his childhood, his intact family.

We stayed on until summer, but I knew I needed a new location for a new start. I put the house on the market, and then, seeing a house in town that I wanted, I called the bank for a second mortgage as a down payment, confident that the old house would sell before too long.

For weeks, packing provoked a little-boy volcano of shouts, angry tears, and thrown possessions. Through my own tears, I talked about the good memories we could build at the new house, but he doubted they would come.

Every time he shouted, "I hate you!" I wanted to shout back, "It's not my fault! I didn't ask for this either!" And once, I actually said it.

In his room one afternoon, we browsed through his shelf of books, some of which he'd had since babyhood. An open cardboard box sat on the floor next to us, and as we looked at the titles, I suggested we donate some of them for younger children to enjoy.

"I don't want to get rid of these," he said, putting the books back on their shelf. "I remember these books, and I still like some of them."

"You can keep the ones you want," I said. "Let's just sort through them as we pack."

But as we sat on the floor surrounded by *Primary Cats*, *Guess How Much I Love You*, and B*rown Bear, Brown Bear*, the tears started rolling down his cheeks.

"I feel like I keep losing things," he gasped raggedly.

With my heart breaking, I hugged him, breathing in the humid scent of little boy sweat and tears as if I could extract his pain. I told him he could keep all the books, knowing that he meant something more. My son had lost his innocence, but there was nothing I could do to bring it back. Even if we stayed in this house, he and I would both be different.

We did move, and Cody's anger followed us to our new house, but with talk and time, it has gotten better. As it turned out, no one wanted to buy our old house in the flood zone. After a year on the market and two years with tenants who left holes in the drywall, I heard about another federal buy-out grant. I applied for it at the end of 2016 and learned in early 2017 that I had been approved at the first stage. For two more years, I paid both mortgages and the flood insurance, hoping that the final approvals would come any day. But each hurricane that hit the US took federal personnel and resources, which delayed my buy-out, and each time Fishing Creek rose, my heart sank, fearing another flood.

Finally, in December 2018, I received a draft of the settlement statement and a closing date for early January. My son, now thirteen, had had years to prepare and mature, but I knew it would still be hard to say goodbye to his childhood home.

At this age, he was so much like his father, the same brown hair, the same cheeks, the same cleft in his chin. Even the same sarcastic sense of humor. But his emotionality he got from me.

Once, when he was nine and I instructed him that throwing clean laundry on his bedroom floor was not a suitable alternative to putting it away in drawers, he replied with outrage, "Why can't you just let me live my own life!" Months later, when I reminded him of this exchange, he dryly remarked, "Huh, I must've been drunk that day!" You could see both his parents in this exchange.

✦ ✦ ✦

"Can we go there one more time?" he asked about our old house. "Can I take something to remember it by?"

"I think that's a good idea," I said.

So, one Saturday before the closing date, I grabbed a screwdriver, some pliers, and a hammer, and my son and I drove over to the old house. Blair had to work at their part-time pizza shop job that day and said we should go without them. We solemnly surveyed each of the cold, empty rooms, now thinly coated with dust. The mood was sad and respectful, like a funeral.

The keepsake my son chose was his bedroom doorknob, made of old, tarnished bronze, probably the house's original. He took the screwdriver from my hand and, with tears in his eyes, removed it himself, the longed-for opening into an inaccessible past.

✦ ✦ ✦

Today, the three of us live in a subdivision built into the side of a mountain. Each week, my children spend half of their time with their respective fathers and the other half, together, with me. Our domestic arrangement is unusual, but we are largely happy. On our best days, I feel that the three of us fit together like the systems of some healthy, clever, joyful organism. The new house isn't perfect—settling has led to uneven floors and some cracks in the ceilings, but I like it.

It sits high above the river, so high up I'm sure it will never flood.

Acknowledgments

I gratefully acknowledge those who helped me revise and improve this book: John Barrett, Critique Circle readers, Mark Decker, Lisa Duff, Dwonna Goldstone, Cristina Mathews, Bob Matthews, MJ Moss, Matt Perakovich, Cherie Randall, Carol Stanley, Deno Trakas, and Jerry Wemple. Thanks also to Andrea Guffey, George Hovis, and Carol Weir for reading and encouraging, and thanks to Bloomsburg University, especially the College of Liberal Arts, for financial assistance.

About the Author

TINA ENTZMINGER is a Southern-born writer and English professor, currently living and working in Pennsylvania. A quadruple divorcee and mother of two teenagers, Entzminger holds a Ph.D. in English from the University of North Carolina at Chapel Hill. Her academic publications include two books: *The Belle Gone Bad: White Southern Women Writers and the Dark Seductress* (LSU Press, 2001) and *Contemporary Reconfigurations of American Literary Classics* (Routledge, 2012) and many essays on American literature.

She loves traveling, gardening, southern history, genealogy, animals, and antiques. She is also a feminist who loves men.

CPSIA information can be obtained
at www.ICGtesting.com
Printed in the USA
BVHW090515231221
624565BV00007B/160